365
EROTIC
SECRETS

for
sensational
sex

365 EROTIC SECRETS

for sensational sex

the ultimate guide to sexual fantasy | DR. PAM SPURR

Amorata Press

Published in the United States by
AMORATA PRESS
an imprint of Ulysses Press
P.O. Box 3440
Berkeley, CA 94703
www.amoratapress.com

First published in the United Kingdom in 2006 as *Sensational Sex* by Robson
Books, an imprint of Anova Books Company Ltd

ISBN10: 1-56975-644-9
ISBN13: 978-1-56975-644-7
Library of Congress Catalog Number: 2007906124

Editorial and production: Claire Chun, Judith Metzener, Elyce Petker
Design: what!design @ whatweb.com

Printed in Canada by Transcontinental Printing

10 9 8 7 6 5 4 3 2 1

Distributed by Publishers Group West

For Nick, thank you for being mine.

Contents

	Acknowledgments	viii
	Sensational and Safer Sex	ix
1	Let the Revolution Begin—Do You Think You Have a Sex Problem?	1
2	Becoming a Sensational Lover!	22
3	Sensational Seduction	39
4	Sensational Sex Talk	66
5	Sensational Foreplay	77
6	Sensational Oral Pleasure	100
7	Sensational Sex Positions	133
8	Sensational Fantasy Play	163
9	Sensationally Advanced Sex-play	189
10	Sensational Lotions, Potions and Playthings	244
11	Sensational Sex Games	270
	The SQ Quiz—Your Sex Quotient	285
	Further Information	289
	About the Author	294

Acknowledgments

Warmest thanks to everyone who has talked candidly to me about their sex lives and experiences. Without your stories, feelings and opinions it would have been impossible to write this book. I'd also like to acknowledge the many friends who've shared personal anecdotes with me about their sex lives and relationships—these have been very helpful in deciding what sex tips and techniques to include.

Thanks as always to Jeremy Robson for his enthusiasm and support and to Barbara Phelan for her skillful editing.

Finally, although this book may appear to be exclusively for straight singles and couples, I'd like to acknowledge the many gay, lesbian and bisexual people who've shared their stories with me. I hope that any person of any sexual orientation will get some benefit or pleasure from the suggestions in this book.

Sensational and Safer Sex

It is extremely important for your sexual health and emotional well-being that you understand the message of safer and responsible sex. As an author, I cannot take responsibility for this aspect of your life.

There are a few main aspects to safer sex you need to consider. First, do not leave safer-sex issues up to a lover. You should know about using condoms and other methods promoting safer sex. If you don't, read the condom packet carefully so that you do know. You should be able to ask any lover to use condoms and if they won't then they aren't someone you should be sleeping with. After all if they don't care about your sexual health then they probably haven't cared for their own.

If you're not confident with condoms, you can read my Condom Confidence tips in Chapter 7. Furthermore you should understand that you are at risk of contracting an STI (sexually transmitted infection) during oral and/or anal sex practices too if you don't use safer-sex methods. These are outlined in Chapter 6 for oral sex and Chapter 9 for anal sex.

If you've been with your lover for some time and want to stop using condoms, you should both go for an STI screen at a sexual health clinic. This will give you the all-clear to stop using condoms and start using other methods of birth control, unless you're planning to get pregnant. Alternatively, if one/both of you has an STI, you can receive the appropriate treatment while you continue to use condoms.

As well as your sexual health, you should consider issues about your emotional well-being if choosing to sleep with someone you don't know. Always exercise caution when looking for a new sexual partner. To become a sensational lover you need to think through all aspects of your new or established sexual relationship, and that includes these very important issues of health and well-being.

ONE

Let the Revolution Begin—Do You Think You Have a Sex Problem?

L et's begin as we mean to go on—with complete honesty—and get right to the heart of the problem with sex! Before I take you through a wealth of sex techniques to try in the coming chapters, I'd like you to start thinking about a couple of important issues. My purpose here is not to outline a detailed theory of human sexuality, but to get you to sit up and evaluate your attitudes toward sex that may be preventing you from having sensational sex. I'll do this by running a revolutionary idea or two past you.

I'd like to know if you'd answer "Yes" to any of the following questions:

- Do you feel inadequate when it comes to sex?
- Do you believe you have a problem with sex of some type?
- Have you been made to feel that something is wrong with you sexually? Or maybe that something's not right between you and your lover?
- After sex do you wonder where the pleasure's gone?
- As a man, do you lose your erection sometimes? Or maybe at times you can't get one?
- Does the thought of sex actually turn you off, when once upon a time it might've turned you on? Or do you find you get aroused but then you can't fully enjoy sex?

If you answered "Yes" to any of these, or similar questions, I'm sure you think you have a genuine sex problem. However, I want you to know right now that I doubt if you have one. Yes, that's about the most important message about sex that you can ever come to accept and understand! Once and for all, we're going to sort out this negative state of affairs, where you believe you have a sex problem. When I say "sex problem" many sex researchers, therapists and experts will say "sexual dysfunction." But as you probably use the term sex problem, from here on in when I use that term I also mean sexual dysfunction.

Perhaps, if you're lucky, you don't feel that you have a sex problem and you're reading *365 Erotic Secrets for Sensational Sex* simply to improve your sex life. I will of course help you to do this with absolutely loads of sensational sex tricks, tips and ideas. But what I have to say in this introductory chapter is important for you too, so keep reading and don't skip to the next chapter. I'd go so far as to say that right now I'm cracking my leather fetish whip insisting you don't skip chapters!

I'm going to outline my revolutionary approach to sex for you—an approach that turns our thinking about sex and sex problems on its head. And it really is that straightforward—you need to turn your thinking around by 180 degrees when it comes to how you view sex, because it is the belief that you have a sex problem that ruins sexual enjoyment in 99 percent of cases. If you follow my revolutionary approach, it will greatly increase your chances to enjoy sensational sex.

This is incredibly important; I can't emphasize this point enough, because when people start talking about so-called "sex problems," believing they have one, they create issues where (in the majority of cases) they don't exist.

Sex problems versus sex symptoms

Putting aside medical problems that may lead to side effects including a Sex Symptom, problems specific to sexual function are in fact rare. For example, it's rare for a woman or man to have nerve damage in their genitals that prevents them from feeling sexually aroused or prevents sexual fulfillment. Equally, for example, it's unusual for a man or a woman to have damage to the nerve pathways in their brain that prevents impulses of sexual arousal getting to important brain centers. Believe me, there are very few real sex problems that originate in the genitals or the nerve pathways up to, and into, the brain centers of sexual pleasure. Except, of course, those things that are the symptoms of something else going on in your life.

So just what are you experiencing when you're either not in the mood for sex, or lose interest in sex, or lose your erection once you get started, or feel that it's pointless, or are physically uncomfortable, or are embarrassed about it? What you're experiencing is what I've come to call a Sex Symptom.

What you, your partner, your best friend, even a sex expert presently call a "sex problem" (or sexual dysfunction) is usually the symptom of something else impacting your sexual enjoyment. These "something elses" form a vast list. They include—but are not limited to—the following:

- Stress—either at work or in your personal life and/or relationship. Unresolved stress can diminish your sex drive and affect your sexual function as a man or a woman. It can also lead to all sorts of other symptoms, such as headaches, stomachaches, backaches and insomnia.

- Overwork—very long hours are a truly modern phenomenon—they can lead to fatigue, loss of appetite, energy and libido.

- Relationship difficulties and problems that may leave you feeling insecure with your partner, or angry at and resentful of them, and definitely not in the mood to sleep with them!

- Bad memories of awkward or unpleasant sex.
- Let's not forget lifestyle choices like drinking too much or taking drugs that can upset the delicate balance of your body chemistry that in turn affect sexual function.
- Smoking is a lifestyle choice that distinctly impacts sexual function.
- Other lifestyle choices like having weight issues that decrease your energy levels and leave you feeling insecure about your attractiveness.
- Then there are the side effects of medications you may be taking for medical problems like diabetes, depression or heart disease that affect sexual feeling and performance. Some medical problems themselves may actually lead to poor blood circulation that in turn may affect your ability to get aroused.
- Finally, I'd like to include your social attitudes that affect your emotional reaction to sex. If you were brought up by parents who said sex was dirty, or sexual feelings were something to be ashamed of, then you'll feel wary about letting go and enjoying sex. The problem is your attitude! The Sex Symptom is your inability to relax in, and enjoy, a sexual experience.

Any of these lifestyle issues, problems and choices, as well as actual medical problems, may lead to a multitude of Sex Symptoms. For example, when you're actually too tired for sex because you've been working long hours—the problem is your choice to work long hours. The Sex Symptom is decreased libido, that is, your sexual energy. Note I say "your choice." That's because we all have choices in our lives, even if at times it doesn't feel that way. Many of the problems that result in various symptoms, including Sex Symptoms, are due to choices that can be changed.

That's one of the first things I'd like you to take from *365 Erotic Secrets for Sensational Sex*—that you can change and have control over your sex life!

Treat the symptom or the problem?

Treat the symptoms of any problem and you rarely get an adequate solution. But treat the root problem and you'll find the symptoms—in this case Sex Symptoms—disappearing. Would a good doctor treat, for example, heart problems just by controlling the symptoms of high blood pressure with blood-pressure medication? Or would they get their patient to make organic changes to their diet and exercise regime, alongside medication? A good doctor would do the latter rather than simply medicating the symptoms! The choice is yours too—treat the actual problem or treat the symptoms. Also, when a doctor says a patient's problem is, for example, diabetes, they say one of the symptoms is frequent urination (micturition). They don't say the patient has a "urination problem." In this case they treat the diabetes and the excessive frequency of urination diminishes.

Let's look at the example of modern parenthood that's fraught with many problems that lead to Sex Symptoms. From the mother's perspective, she may be sore for a few weeks after the birth as well as being exhausted. If she's breast-feeding, her nipples may be very sensitive. She may also have what I call "cuddle-fatigue" where she's been holding her baby all day and simply doesn't want to be touched that much by her partner. Then there's "baby-interruptus" where even if you start feeling a little sexy, your baby starts crying and your sexy mood abruptly changes. From the father's perspective, he may also be exhausted and, if there isn't good communication, may feel shut out from the mother–baby duo.

In this example, she may feel useless as a lover and he may start feeling resentful toward his partner. In turn, neither feels much sexual arousal. This lack of sexual arousal is the Sex Symptom for both of them.

Should such parents tackle the problem or the Sex Symptoms? Quite frankly, just looking at their lack of sexual arousal is not going to solve things between them in a meaningful way! You'd be better off starting with the problem.

The problem can be split into the practical aspects like those of fatigue and soreness. One solution would be rescheduling their daily life and building in nap times to help with fatigue, and doing "baby-shares" with other couples as babysitters to give them quality time off. She could see her doctor about any ongoing soreness; he might recommend various lubricants and exercises.

On the emotional side of their problems, where misunderstandings have resulted from poor communication, they could agree to sit down and talk through point-by-point what's working in their new life as a family unit and what's not working so well, then set goals to change these. They could use different communication techniques to rebuild trust and belief in each other.

Therefore, by picking apart the actual problems such a couple faces, they'll soon realize that the lack of sexual enjoyment is simply the Sex Symptom of their real problems. Even if it didn't originally feel like this and felt much more personal and threatening. Practical steps can often solve such problems leading to enhanced sexual enjoyment and the Sex Symptoms disappear.

☙ SENSATIONAL SEX SECRET

Many new mothers do not feel sexy for six to twelve months after the birth of a child. However, relationship research shows that if a man gets romantic, he greatly increases his chances of rekindling sexual desire in his partner. Time to brush up on your sensual massage technique and get some romantic candles out if you're a new dad!

Do we need to distinguish between a problem and a sex symptom?

You may think this distinction between a problem and a Sex Symptom is NOT that important but believe me, it is vastly important. When people think they have a sex problem they experience a whole set of negative emotions. They might feel ashamed, guilty, angry, frustrated, inhibited, undesirable, unattractive, useless, threatened and vulnerable, and more. If such feelings persist, they can be carried over into other areas of life and even future relationships, and can jeopardize present relationships.

To be labeled or to label yourself as having a sex problem goes right to the core of your belief in yourself, your desirability and attractiveness, and even your personality—whether you'll be thought to have an exciting, interesting and sexy personality. By labeling something like stress as a "sex problem," not only is it harder to solve but it also complicates issues leading to loss of self-esteem, and potentially a sense of failure, shame and guilt—extremely damaging feelings for intimate relationships.

We can change every one of these negative, unpleasant feelings by accepting that what we see as sex problems are usually Sex Symptoms as I've described. Realizing that the problem lies elsewhere, and simply impacts our sexual enjoyment, can be a great relief.

For example, if you can say you have a problem with long hours at work that negatively impact your life, you need to restructure and reprioritize your work. I'd like you to consider what feels better at a personal level to claim as your problem: long work hours or having a poor sex life? And what makes more sense? It makes more sense to claim and solve the real problem. Problems are always solved more easily when people don't feel personally threatened by them.

This is particularly true when we live in a society so permeated with sex that it seems like the be-all and end-all of how we compare ourselves to others. You only need to think about how, when sex comes up as a topic of conversation with your friends or at work, all sorts of thoughts run through your mind. Thoughts like "I'm not as good at it as they are," or "My sex life isn't like that," or even "No way! I didn't know such things existed!"

Yes, to have sensational sex is bliss but there are many ways of having blissful experiences. You'll prevent yourself from having sensational sex if you buy into the notion that you have a sex problem when only a small percentage of people actually have sex problems. Instead, I hope you now see that what you're experiencing is probably a Sex Symptom. Always check with your doctor though, if you think you have a medical problem.

After so-called sex problems come sex myths!

It is my aim to right many of the wrongs that lead people to feel they're abnormal and not up to par as lovers. From talking to thousands of people over the years in my various roles, I firmly believe that there are many damaging myths which need to be exploded around sex and sexual behavior. Many of these sex myths are linked to the belief that you have a so-called sex problem if you aren't having sex as per these sex myths. I'll outline some of the most damaging myths here and then in forthcoming chapters raise the issue of sex myths where relevant. Sex myths can be defined as those things we take as a given or a truth, without questioning them.

MAJOR MYTH 1: WOMEN REACH ORGASM THROUGH PENETRATIVE SEX

Let's begin with the main myth surrounding a woman's ability to reach orgasm. A woman who can't reach orgasm, or can only reach it sometimes, or has difficulty reaching it through penetration, is considered to have a sex problem. But this buys into the myth that it's easy for women to reach orgasm through penetrative sex and that is simply not true!

This myth perpetuates the belief that it's "normal" for women to orgasm during penetrative sex. However, this is blatantly untrue, since by far the majority of women are NOT able to orgasm during penetrative sex. It is the very lucky thirty percent who can either occasionally or frequently reach orgasm during penetrative sex that are ABNORMAL—and lucky to be so. I don't like using the words normal and abnormal; however, we tend to judge what is acceptable against the majority of people and then classify this as normal.

MAJOR MYTH 2: WOMEN SHOULD REACH ORGASM MORE EASILY THROUGH PENETRATIVE SEX THAN ORAL SEX

A further sex myth we buy into is that it's actually "normal" to achieve orgasm more easily through penetrative sex rather than through oral sex for the majority of women. In fact, if given the chance, women orgasm more readily through oral sex where the pressure and friction is easier to control than in penetrative sex.

♭ SENSATIONAL SEX SECRET

Try the Magic Swirl—Without touching her clitoris directly, swirl your tongue around it, varying the speed and intensity. She will find this absolute bliss.

MAJOR MYTH 3: MEN WANT MORE SEX THAN WOMEN

The same is true for male sex myths of which there are many. Let me tackle a couple of critical ones here. By far the majority of men buy into the belief that they'll be more highly sexed than a female partner. They consider themselves abnormal and to have sex problems if they aren't. In fact the reverse is true, as many studies show that once in a relationship, women often continue to want more frequent sex than their male partners. You ARE normal if you find that your partner wants more sex than you do!

MAJOR MYTH 4: REAL MEN DON'T LOSE THEIR ERECTIONS

The fact that most men at some point will lose their erection is often ignored. Instead, men are fed the myth that if they ever lose their erection then there's something lacking in their masculinity and levels of virility. The implication is that this is a major sex problem. This simply isn't true! As with so-called sex problems, the loss of an erection is usually a Sex Symptom of something like being overtired, being nervous, having an adverse reaction to medication, or having had too much to drink. The majority of men have been guilty of, for example, having drunk too much on occasion and thus experience "brewer's droop." This does not mean they're not masculine or virile!

On the other hand, getting back to the difference between a problem and a Sex Symptom, if they persistently drank and lost their erection, then they'd need to look at the root problem causing them to drink which resulted in the Sex Symptom of erectile dysfunction (ED).

I hope this gives you food for thought about buying into any sex myths when you should always question them. People who enjoy the most sensational sex are those who find what works for them. They do NOT worry about what they think the rest of the population is doing.

Sex symptom checklist

To give you an idea of the extent of any lifestyle or health issues you need to address since they could result in Sex Symptoms, I'd like you to complete the following Sex Symptom checklist honestly.

1. Do you work more than a 40-hour week?   Yes / No
2. Do you worry about your work when you
    get home?   Yes / No
3. Do you feel you lack control over your career? Yes / No
4. Do you lose sleep over your work?   Yes / No
5. Do you drink or take drugs to unwind?   Yes / No
6. Do you have money worries?   Yes / No
7. Do you find it hard to get day-to-day jobs
    done because of lack of time or energy?   Yes / No
8. Do you have any ongoing health issues?   Yes / No
9. Do you take any medication?   Yes / No
10. Do you have trouble sleeping for any reason?   Yes / No
11. Do you have any ongoing disputes with
    family or friends?   Yes / No
12. Have you been bereaved in the last six months? Yes / No
13. Are you single and unhappy about it?   Yes / No
14. Do you think you're unattractive in any way?   Yes / No
15. Do you worry what a lover will think about you? Yes / No
16. Do you have young, attention-demanding
    children?   Yes / No

17. If in a relationship, do you and your partner have
    any ongoing issues outside of the bedroom?   Yes / No
18. Do you find it hard to communicate with
    your partner?   Yes / No
19. Do you worry about pleasing your partner
    in bed?   Yes / No
20. Do you have issues with your weight or
    body image?   Yes / No

Key: If you've answered "Yes" to any of the above you could be experiencing Sex Symptoms! It only takes one of these everyday areas to affect your sex life, so it's time to sort it out. This is part of the overall aim of *365 Erotic Secrets for Sensational Sex*—to get you thinking about how sexual pleasure and fulfillment fits into your whole life and lifestyle.

If you can address any one of your Sex Symptoms and not think of it as a sex problem with all the "emotional baggage" attached to that, then you should be able to move forward quickly in solving it. Remember that revolutionizing your thinking in terms of Sex Symptoms frees you from all the negativity associated in our society with sex problems.

365 Erotic Secrets for Sensational Sex is all about helping you to enjoy your sexual experiences and find sexual fulfillment—it's important for you to revolutionize your thinking about so-called "sex problems" because most people (and this includes you) believe that at some point in their relationships, they've experienced a sex problem. This simply isn't true and it's damaging to believe this. Thinking you have a so-called sex problem simply magnifies any feelings of insecurity or inadequacy you have.

Here I'd like to outline a format for you that'll help you reframe your thinking about the Sex Symptoms you may be experiencing now or in the future. This format can be applied to the majority of Sex Symptoms. I'd like to remind you that what I call a Sex Symptom covers anything that makes you anxious or concerned about your sex life. Sex Symptoms should be examined within the framework of the following four levels. This will help you to *logically* think through what is in fact a highly emotionally charged area.

LEVEL 1: MEDICAL ISSUES

You first need to examine whether any illness or medical problem you have, or have had, has interfered with your sexual satisfaction or ability to sustain sexual activity. You also need to look at any medication you're taking that may affect sex drive or the ability to sustain sexual activity.

If you have any suspicions whatsoever that medication or a medical problem is affecting your sex life then you MUST consult your doctor. Hopefully, such a consultation will answer your questions and give you a perspective on the situation. For example, your doctor may tell you that the medication you're presently on affects libido. He or she may suggest changing it or reviewing it at some future point. If your doctor diagnoses a long-term condition such as diabetes, for example, you'll have to talk through how this will affect your sexual enjoyment and what the medical options are to sustain enjoyment. You may find as a woman that your lack of sexual arousal is actually due to some changes in nerve function during childbirth or through some other gynecological procedure. Again, in these rare circumstances you'll need to talk through the treatment options with your doctor.

If you're satisfied that your Sex Symptoms do not relate to any medical issue, you can take this off the list of potential reasons for your lack of sexual enjoyment.

LEVEL 2: PSYCHOLOGICAL AND EMOTIONAL ISSUES

It's important now to explore any psychological or emotional issues that may be the real problem behind your Sex Symptoms. The questions you need to ask yourself include whether you could be experiencing, for example, depression, anxiety or chronic stress? Perhaps you have a fear or phobia that's causing you anxiety and this anxiety has spread into every aspect of your life including the bedroom? Or maybe you have non-specific fears, such as social phobias, that are causing you generalized anxiety?

Could it be long-standing negative feelings established in your childhood that make you feel insecure or inadequate? Maybe you experienced the trauma of childhood sexual abuse that has left you with a sense of shame and guilt that permeates your very being?

These and any other psychological and emotional issues of long-standing, or indeed recent emotional problems like bereavement, can greatly impact your sexual desire and experience.

If any of these examples ring true for you or make you realize that you may be experiencing something similar, then you'll need to take appropriate action to sort it out and work on healing yourself. If you haven't been able to heal yourself then maybe you need professional counseling-type help.

This is a good time to "think in ink" and write down in a notebook the sorts of worries and negative feelings that affect you on a day-to-day basis. You can then start to challenge negative feelings and thoughts on a daily basis. Take one day at a time, and when an unpleasant thought comes into your head, challenge it and think of positive examples that combat it. Make time to research the best method of positive thinking for you—there are countless books and websites on the subject.

LEVEL 3: RELATIONSHIP ISSUES

Any friction or problem in your relationship can lead to Sex Symptoms. It might be the case that you and your partner have long-standing disagreements, for example over finances or how to spend your free time, or you've just recently argued over something. Either way, it may affect your feelings toward each other, leading to Sex Symptoms.

Rationally, it's not hard to work out that if you're fuming about an issue with your partner (either privately or you're both very much aware of angry feelings) or arguing about an area of your life together, you're not going to feel like hopping into bed with them. However, people often fail to recognize that a relationship problem outside the bedroom can diminish their sexual desire or enjoyment. For some reason they don't link the two and just wonder why they don't feel like sex.

It's important that relationship problems/issues are met head on and not swept under the carpet. It's so easy to think that if you ignore a problem, it'll go away. What's more than likely to happen is that you'll develop symptoms of the festering issue. And these may well be Sex Symptoms.

Start by acknowledging what's working well between you two. It may be the case that when you're out visiting friends you can still have a laugh together. But at home you constantly argue over who should do what around the house. By generating a positive vibe about the good moments you can then tackle the things that are getting you down.

From this positive starting point you can move on to the more difficult issues. As this is not a relationship book, I'm not going to go into the details here. However, if you refer to Chapter 4 on talking about sex, there are many tips there for good communication that can be used in practically any arena.

LEVEL 4: LIFESTYLE ISSUES

The final issues you need to examine are your lifestyle choices that have the potential to result in Sex Symptoms. As mentioned earlier in this chapter, when I was kick-starting your new way of thinking about your sex life, people make all sorts of lifestyle choices that impact the rest of their life. How can you, for example, drink a bottle of wine each night and not expect it to affect your blood circulation, in turn affecting your ability to get sexually aroused. As a man, this would mean not being able to get an erection, or as a woman not feeling particularly aroused by foreplay, thinking you have a sex problem.

If you stopped drinking, as a woman your sexual sensations would come back and as a man your erections would too (as long as you hadn't damaged your circulatory system permanently). But instead you're still thinking you have a sex problem rather than acknowledging you have a lifestyle problem that's giving you a Sex Symptom.

Let's take this back a step. Let's say that you drink a bottle of wine each night because you're very stressed at work. You believe that you don't know how to deal with it because you haven't thought through coping strategies. That stress leads you to drink too much—your lifestyle choice. Alternative lifestyle choices would be to deal with that stress in more positive and appropriate ways. Then you wouldn't have any Sex Symptoms.

This is true of any lifestyle choice that impacts you physically or mentally. Such lifestyle choices include your decision to exhaust yourself, for example, playing poker games on the Internet for four hours each evening after work; or choosing to work very long hours because you want to have the money for a bigger car. Lifestyle choices also include things like smoking or eating too much, or taking recreational drugs. Perhaps you're burning the candle at both ends, working hard and then going out many evenings each week playing hard. You simply end up too tired for sex.

These and many other things are lifestyle choices that will negatively impact your sexual desire or stamina. You need to sort out what choices you're making that have such detrimental effects.

Ultimately, it's important that everyone examine these four levels of their life. Not simply for their sexual enjoyment but generally for their well-being across all areas of their life.

And now let's turn our attention to the next couple of important things to consider on your way to becoming a sensational lover.

TWO

Becoming a Sensational Lover!

You and your pleasure are the focus of this chapter. Now that you have begun to revolutionize your thinking about so-called "sex problems" and Sex Symptoms, it's time to get you started along the road to becoming a sensational self-lover.

The most important ingredients to enjoying sexual pleasure and being a sensational lover are these: know your own body and your own mind. Many sex experts and writers simply advise learning new techniques, but it's absolutely important that we revolutionize your thinking and start with your body and your mind. Therefore, this chapter is going to be all about you, yes wonderful, sexy you! And if you don't feel that way at the moment, you can certainly learn how.

Think of yourself as a novice, yet revolutionary explorer and that your body is a rich and undiscovered country. Even someone who is highly sexually experienced can neglect, or leave unexplored, various erogenous zones. There are always new sensations to create and enjoy, and new techniques to try. But this is all down to the way you think and how much you know your body. I know you're dying for some sensational sex suggestions (and I have so many coming up in the following chapters) but you have to do the groundwork if you're going to be a sensational lover. Unfortunately, we've come to expect instant results for everything from ordering pizza to satisfying our sex lives. However, patience and understanding will take you the whole sensational way.

The way you think

We tend to use the phrase "it's all in your mind" as a negative. A good example is when a lover is accused of flirting outside the relationship. You can just hear the accused "Flirt" reply, "It's all in your mind, I wouldn't flirt with anyone else!" People use this saying as a put down and to lessen the impact of what someone is thinking. However, when it comes to the way you think about sex, it's a positive saying.

Your sensuality and sexiness are quite frankly all in your mind. I have discussed this many times in my other books and articles. It's now well recognized that the brain is the biggest sex organ. If your mind is not engaged in a sexual experience, it won't happen. For example, as a man you could have two gorgeous lap dancers gyrating in front of you and you still wouldn't get aroused if your mind was elsewhere. As a woman, I could put Brad Pitt at your feet, in a tiny thong, and it wouldn't set your pulse racing. This is because your mind is so powerful that if it has things other than sex on it, it'll prevent your body getting aroused. Let's quickly run through the stages of getting aroused.

The stages of sexual desire and arousal

Without going into unnecessary physiological detail, I'd like to run you through the basics of sexual desire and arousal. I don't go into the various things that may occur at any point. However, by understanding that your mind needs to be "available," that's a big start in understanding how hiccups might occur at any stage of desire or arousal. For example, you may look across the room at your lover and desire them, but if you also catch sight of the stack of papers on your desk, then work issues will take over your mind and interrupt the stage of initial desire. Or maybe your partner and you have felt desire and started caressing each other to the point that you're feeling physically aroused, but at that moment your baby wakes and cries, and your mind immediately switches off sexual arousal. And so it goes at any stage of desire and arousal and orgasm, except, of course, if you've reached the "point of no return" for orgasm when not even an earthquake will stop it!

Unlike a car that can go from 0–60 mph in seconds, our bodies work in another way, and as individuals they each function very differently. On average (and you know I hate this word "average" as much as the word "normal," but for simplicity's sake I'll use it. I'd like you to know that I don't see your experiences as necessarily being average or normal!), for a woman it takes roughly 25–28 minutes to build up to orgasm, and for a man it takes approximately 10–12 minutes. These timings vary between individuals so a highly orgasmic woman may climax very quickly, and some men take longer to reach orgasm than their partners.

Different sex researchers discuss the stages of desire through to orgasm in varying ways. To keep things simple I'll run through all the stages mentioned by different researchers.

STAGE 1: SEX DRIVE

We talk about sex drive as if everyone has the same level, but sex drive varies a great deal from those who have very little or no sex drive to those who would be considered to have a very high drive.

A person's sex drive helps define the way they see themselves sexually. That in turn affects the way they relate to a lover. If you view yourself as "highly sexed" you may be quite frustrated with a partner you see as having a low sex drive. Couples often report "problems" with varying levels of sex drive between them but usually a successful compromise can be reached if they keep calm about the situation. It can be very difficult if, for example, your partner has accused you of being "a nymphomaniac," or on the other hand "frigid," because either you have a higher or lower sex drive than they do.

♨ SENSATIONAL SEX SECRET

Calling a lover any negative, derisive or thoughtless name will worsen the situation when you're facing a Sex Symptom. So bite your tongue if you're angry or unhappy.

Sex drive is definitely affected by what's on your mind, your physical health and well-being, whether you're hungry, tired, drunk and many other factors. Over time your sex drive will fluctuate depending on your circumstances and commonly, as you get older, your sex drive tends to diminish.

STAGE 2: SEXUAL DESIRE

We've established you have to have some sort of sex drive to even get going. The next step is feeling desire. Since 99 percent of the time, desire begins in your mind, this is also a complicated stage. If your mind doesn't desire someone, or some activity, your body will rarely follow into the next stage. A good example of this is going out on the "pull." People tell me that they might've been feeling highly sexed and felt desire for the person they took home on the night they hooked up. But on waking and looking at the person they picked up, they think, "What on earth was I thinking?" In the morning they simply do not feel desire for the person who looked desirable the night before with beer goggles on!

Your mind has to be involved for you to feel desire. But that's why, when their mind is altered by the influence of alcohol, people make decisions they wouldn't make when sober.

Any one of your senses may be pricked with desire. For example, your sense of touch as your partner gently brushes past you; your sense of hearing when you hear a romantic or sexy song; your sense of smell when your partner comes in from the gym with fresh perspiration—chock-full of pheromones!—and, of course, your sense of sight when you see something that you consider sexy. When your desire is stimulated you're able to go through to the next stage unless, of course, you're interrupted.

♭ SENSATIONAL SEX SECRET

Pretend you haven't noticed that your blouse has fallen open and allow your lover to catch a glimpse of cleavage. Or you can bend over so they sneak a peek of your panties. This visual stimulation will excite their desire.

STAGE 3: AROUSAL

Sexual arousal is the stage when your body catches up with your mind's desire. This can occur with surprising speed. A man only needs to catch a glimpse of a woman's cleavage to get the beginnings of blood rushing to his penis. A woman only needs to brush her breasts gently against a man's shoulder to have her nipples become erect. As physical arousal increases, your genitalia engorge with blood, lubrication begins, your breathing gets shallower, muscles tense with anticipation, etc. Whatever you wish to call it, these signs show you're feeling horny.

♦ SENSATIONAL SEX SECRET

Prolong the arousal stage and you'll have a more intense orgasm! Those who rush through foreplay thinking they can't wait to climax miss out on the fact that the longer the plateau stage (when you're aroused but not ready to peak), 99 percent of the time, the better the orgasm.

The arousal stage is complex and we shouldn't underestimate the different influences on it. On the emotional side, you may feel desire for your new lover, but if you were told by an ex-lover that you were lousy in bed, fear of a repeat of this prevents your body from catching up with your mind's desire. As a woman, this may show itself in the fact that you don't get vaginal lubrication and so penetration is painful. But as another example to show the range of effects on the arousal stage, a woman may not get vaginal lubrication due to a hormonal imbalance despite wanting to make love to her partner. Or a man who drinks and smokes heavily may like his partner but finds that he doesn't get physically aroused due to circulatory problems.

If arousal progresses nicely, without interruption, you'll be ready for the next stage. Although this doesn't necessarily mean you'll reach it.

⚓ SENSATIONAL SEX SECRET

If you're a man who's worried about why you're not getting aroused and wants to explore whether there's an emotional or physical basis, try this postage-stamp test. Before you go to bed, take a ring of postage stamps and paste them around the base of your penis. If it's pulled and snapped in the night you'll know you've had a nocturnal erection. This means your lack of erection may have an emotional basis.

STAGE 4: ORGASM

Over the years as a relationship expert, I've had the chance to ask hundreds of men and women to describe what an orgasm feels like. What strikes me is that people use very different descriptive words. For example, some describe them as flowing, shocking or electrifying, and also report that their orgasms vary. Sometimes they're intense, sometimes mellow and all points in between. So your orgasm will be very different to someone else's and will also differ from time to time.

Add to that the fact that you'll reach orgasm at very different rates. Many women and some men experience a "plateau" where they are highly aroused but it takes time for them to reach a threshold where they cross over into orgasm. Frequently men (and their partners) wish that they could control their "plateau" longer so that the woman is allowed to catch up, as on the whole men are quicker.

But the biggest issue with understanding and enhancing your orgasms is the enormous pressure to reach it. This is a modern phenomenon. Ancient sex advice as found in the likes of the Kama Sutra, probably dating from the first century A.D., emphasized the spiritual side of lovemaking. The entire sexual experience was imbued with great potential for the couple to become truly emotionally and physically intimate.

However, nowadays we are so goal-oriented and the orgasm has become the goal. The entire goal! I need to emphasize the importance of enjoying the journey as much as the end result and that you can have sensational sex without reaching orgasm. Sex does not equal orgasm! You'll be far less likely to experience unsatisfactory sex if you learn to appreciate each moment with your lover rather than focusing on getting to orgasm.

♌ SENSATIONAL SEX SECRET

Couples who take the emphasis off orgasm during lovemaking are much more likely to orgasm! The Sensate Focus exercises of the 1970s are still important in this sense. They encouraged people to enjoy each moment of sensual touching and not worry about the end result.

STAGE 5: SATISFACTION AND RESOLUTION

On reaching orgasm there is a final stage of resolution that involves emotional and sexual satisfaction and a return to a normal physical state. Blood leaves the engorged genitals, the muscles relax, and vaginal lubrication ceases. Most men have found that no matter how much they want seconds, particularly with a new partner, it takes on average about twenty minutes for them to become aroused again. In older men this refractory period increases; however, very young men may get erect after only a few minutes. A woman may respond to sensational stimulation from her partner very quickly after orgasm despite her body going through a resolution phase.

My final word about stages is that if you're experiencing Sex Symptoms at any stage—desire, arousal or orgasm—discuss it thoroughly with your doctor.

ℒ SENSATIONAL
SEX SECRET

The "emotional bonding" hormone, oxytocin, is at its peak after orgasm so ensure you cuddle and caress each other to maximize these bonding moments, deepening your relationship.

Time to explore yourself!

Understanding the stages of desire and arousal is important but it's time to get to grips with your body. And I mean this literally. Too many people are hung up about masturbation when it's absolutely the key to becoming a sensational lover. If you don't know how your own body works then how on earth can you expect a lover to work it out? And if you're not good at exploring your own body, how will you be good at getting around someone else's?

You wouldn't expect to climb into a car and just start it, would you? You need to know how it works, tinker with it and explore it. You wouldn't expect to sit behind a PC for the very first time, turn it on, and know how to operate it, would you? You'd read the instruction manual for your new refrigerator, clothes dryer, DVD recorder, etc. So why on earth would you not become a learner-driver for your own body?

I'd actually go so far as to state this as a fact—you can't be a sensational lover without knowing your own body. If you need reassurance, believe me that nearly 100 percent of people have tried masturbating. The famous sex researcher Alfred Kinsey alleged that 98 percent of men in his studies reported masturbating and that the other 2 percent had lied.

☾ SENSATIONAL SEX SECRET

Start simply. Lie back comfortably, take your index finger and gently trace a line from your forehead down over your nose, across your lips, down your chin and on to your neck. Think of the lovely line that your finger has traced on the very fragile skin of your face and neck. Continue this gentle touch and move your fingertips back around the sensitive skin of your ear lobes. Moisten your fingertip by sucking it gently and then allow your finger to trail all over your body.

GETTING STARTED

If you find the idea of exploring your own body daunting, then you need to start in subtle ways. If you go into a sexual encounter feeling this way about your own body then you'll transmit this anxiety in subtle ways to your lover. We always talk about "learning to love yourself" emotionally and this is important because you can then share real love with another. It's the same with learning to love yourself sexually; when you're comfortable with you then you can share this with another person.

YOUR SEXUAL CONFIDENCE

Building your sexual confidence is important in learning to pleasure yourself. Start by using a visualization every day. You'll need to choose one that works for you. For people who aren't used to visualizing, I find this light-hearted one is quite good to get started with. Get warm and comfortable, put on some soothing music and light a candle. Close your eyes and imagine yourself as a sex god or goddess. You'll be wearing flowing, sensual robes made of filmy fabric. A warm sun will be shining on you and you'll be telling yourself you are worth every sensual pleasure in the world.

Take a few minutes each day to relax and enjoy this image as you build the confidence to learn about your body. If you haven't used a visualization before, you may scoff at the notion; however, think about it this way—how much time do you spend worrying each day? I bet you worry a lot more than the few minutes you could spend on a positive visualization! And which makes more sense? Worrying about your new lover and whether or not he or she will have a good time with you in bed, or giving yourself a few moments of confidence-boosting meditation?

SEXUAL CONFIDENCE—THE NEXT LEVEL

Many people experience feelings of guilt about enjoying sex, particularly about learning to pleasure themselves. Why would nature have given us the capability to experience sexual pleasure if we weren't supposed to? Most negative notions about masturbation, and sexual enjoyment generally, come from our parents, teachers, and church leaders. They're simply repeating the mantra that they learned as a child, that you shouldn't touch yourself. You can break that cycle and realize that masturbation is not sad, bad or dirty!

Once you've established yourself as a sex god or sex goddess, you can also start stamping out negative and inhibiting thoughts that might crop up. If, for example, a little voice in your head starts saying, "You shouldn't be doing this!" then learn to turn it on its head. Substitute a thought like, "Of course I can enjoy my body!" Thinking is habitual and it influences how we feel. You can learn to have a positive-thinking habit or to continue with your negative-thinking habit.

OTHER PLACES TO GET COMFORTABLE

Once you've found that masturbation is a positive thing, which is helping you to learn about your body, from time to time you may try somewhere new. The bath or shower is a fantastic place to relax and touch yourself, with water cascading around you. Try your sofa or a big soft easy chair as somewhere to pleasure yourself. Some people enjoy getting a little more daring and sit on the edge of the bed looking into their bedroom mirror while they touch themselves. And for something a little more sensational, why not indulge while sitting in your desk chair in your office (behind locked doors!).

HOW TO TOUCH YOURSELF

Since you have so many different erogenous zones, you may find you want to touch them in different ways. You caress, scratch, tickle, massage, pinch, and "tap" them with your fingertips, hands and wrists. You might also prefer gently massaging yourself with a vibrator. Many women masturbate against a silky pair of panties, as they don't like direct touch of their clitoral region. Some avoid direct touch altogether and pleasure themselves by rubbing against a pillow between their thighs. Others use the palm of their hand. You might ask why on earth you should experiment on yourself with touch? Because experimenting with touch can help you be more imaginative when touching your lover and asking them to touch you.

It's important to remember there isn't a "right" or "wrong" way to masturbate. After touching different parts of your body, you may even prolong sexual release by doing things like gently and slowly pulling at your pubic hair to create a teasing sensation. Or run your fingers back and forth over your pubic bone—like a light touch on the piano. In the bath, you may tease yourself with the showerhead—enjoy the trickling of the water and slowly increase the pressure to where it feels perfect for you. A word of caution: Always point the showerhead downward from the pubic bone and not up into the vagina as otherwise there's a small risk of forcing an air bubble into your bloodstream.

∿ SENSATIONAL SEX SECRET

Once you become skilled at pleasuring yourself you may want to tease your lover and allow him to watch. Lie back in a softly lit room and let go in front of him. Your lover will get incredibly turned on!

SOMETHING FOR THE GIRLS

Quite frankly, men's genitals are on the outside and easier to get to know. Many women tell me they've never even looked at themselves. Get a hand-held mirror and examine all the beautiful parts to your genitals. Look at yourself as if you're an exotic flower. Stop any negative thoughts that your genitals are ugly.

A REMINDER ABOUT SELF-PLEASURE

Just as when you're making love to a partner, masturbation is NOT simply about having an orgasm. It's about the whole package—you, your feelings, your fantasies, knowing your body and more. Also, what you learn about general pleasure and reaching orgasm can then be shared with your lover. Another important point is that you can learn about all your erogenous zones. We don't want to leave any stone unturned in terms of your wealth of "pleasure points" as I like to call them!

YOU AND YOUR LOVER'S EROGENOUS ZONES

Discovering your favorite erogenous zones from your scalp down to your toes is important. But don't forget that everyone responds differently. Stimulation of an erogenous zone that excites one person, for example, gentle stroking of the inner wrist, will feel awful to another.

MALE AND FEMALE EROGENOUS ZONES

Erogenous zones include the scalp, ears, neck, collarbone and shoulders, underarms, arms, elbows, wrists, hands, palms, fingers, breasts and nipples, ribs, abdomen, back, buttocks, hips, genitals, thighs, knees, ankles, feet and toes—and all points in between!

WHEN MASTURBATION BECOMES A PROBLEM

Like any behavior, masturbation can occasionally become a problem, usually becoming compulsive. This is more common in men than women and has little to do with sex. Compulsive masturbation is usually more about relieving stress and anxiety. It becomes a behavior, or habit, that provides temporary relief from anxiety or stress. Compulsive masturbation isn't about choice, as the person feels compelled to do it. This can interfere with the person's relationship or work, and may require professional treatment. Masturbation is a healthy pursuit for most people.

UNDERSTANDING A LOVER

Take everything you've just learned about yourself, then turn it around and think about understanding your lover, or a future lover, in this way. You need to understand their mind and how it can get distracted or stressed, or at other times what arouses and stimulates them. You also need to think about their body and getting to know it like some wonderful, unexplored and exotic foreign country. Before you learn how to do this, you first need to understand the art of seduction and how to attract a lover...

THREE

Sensational Seduction

If you're in a relationship, you may wonder why I think it's important for you to read about sensational seduction techniques. It's important because many couples face the age-old issue of getting into a rut when it comes to their sex life and/or simply taking each other for granted. One way to prevent this from happening is to know the little tricks and techniques to keep things alive. This is a revolutionary way of thinking that will keep your seduction skills fresh and interesting.

It's easy to forget that there's nothing quite so delicious as knowing someone is pursuing you, trying to seduce you. It makes you feel utterly desirable, lifts your spirits and boosts your confidence. If you think you can't do this with a long-standing lover then you need to think again. Acquiring this skill will separate an ordinary relationship from a sensational relationship.

If you're single at present, then you might also need to hone your seduction skills so you can attract someone when the time is right.

Elements of attraction

Research into lust and love shows there are many different factors that conspire to throw us into the arms of one person rather than another. Haven't you sometimes looked at a couple and thought, "How on earth did those two get together?" It's hard to fathom the chemistry between some people, but having a better understanding of the chemistry of seduction and attraction will help to make sense of such odd couplings—and why you might be attracted to someone unexpected!

Over the last five to ten years, researchers have found there are many factors operating to determine whether or not you attract, and seduce, someone. Here are some of these findings in brief:

- Research has shown that when we're attracted to someone, four specific regions of the brain are activated. These give those wonderful symptoms, traditionally called lovesickness, that include euphoria, obsession and butterflies in the stomach.
- Dopamine, the chemical responsible for addiction, is stimulated when couples fall for each other. Dopamine production triggers a feel-good sensation so we want to repeat that sensation by seeing the person again.

- Another intoxicating chemical is Nerve Growth Factor, which causes the telltale palpitations, butterflies and sweaty palms. NGF rises considerably when you're attracted to someone and then tails off after six months—the end of the traditional honeymoon period. Through those exciting sensations, it keeps you interested for long enough to hopefully bond and form a lasting relationship.

- Memory of your first kiss quite literally gets implanted in the amygdala part of the brain, which is responsible for the emotions. Such a dramatic and romantic event is rarely forgotten by someone even twenty, thirty, or forty years later. So try to ensure your first kiss with a new lover is a fantastic one.

- It's been found that at a subconscious level you're attracted to someone who has genes related to the immune system's response, that are different to yours, so that you end up with a good mix if you reproduce. Their MHC molecules (major histo-compatibility complex) give off a smell that we don't notice, but which affects us profoundly.

- Pheromones are also important in attracting a partner. Some of these affect our sense of smell at a subconscious level telling us whether or not we like the person's scent. At other times, we notice this at a very conscious level such as when someone hasn't showered!

❥ In fact having sex can be very time-consuming and exhausting, but it is beneficial to our ability as humans to reproduce as a couple rather than asexually as some organisms do. The harsher and more demanding the environment that you successively reproduce in, the stronger the genes you pass on!

Most of us calculate, largely subconsciously, what the chances are that someone we're attracted to will be attracted back. This calculation then determines whether we pursue them and try to seduce them. But if you revolutionize your thinking about attraction and seduction, and take control of it, then you'll take on board the fact that there's a whole host of things such as those mentioned above, involved in sexual attraction. This will help you understand why it is, or isn't, happening with you and someone else.

A key part of this is establishing that "comfort zone" around you. So when the person you're attracted to is nearby, make them feel good in your presence. And what makes one person feel good might be very different for another person. These various fascinating pieces of research are like pieces of a puzzle. Being aware of this will help you fit the pieces together when you meet someone new whom you want to seduce.

WHAT ALSO ATTRACTS A MAN

Going back to our animal instincts, traditionally a man is attracted to a number of feminine characteristics that signal a woman could bear healthy offspring to ensure his genetic line continues. High round breasts, a trim waistline and rounded hips signal a healthy female. Large doe eyes set high above the cheeks as well as pink lips and cheeks signal youthfulness, which is desirable to mating. Soft, high vocal tones have also been shown to arouse attraction.

Despite this overall "template for femininity" there are differences between men about which attributes attract them most. Some men are "bottom men," some are "breast men" and some are "leg men." Others will go for anything in a skirt!

WHAT ALSO ATTRACTS A WOMAN

Again, in terms of our primal needs for survival, the classic V shape of a man's broader shoulders and narrow waist, which signals they have the muscular strength to hunt and fish, providing food and shelter, traditionally attracts women. During the fertile part of their menstrual cycle, women tend to be attracted to a more masculine face. Later in the cycle they're attracted to a slightly softer but still manly face.

As with men, women are attracted by individual attributes. One woman might choose a very different man to the one her best friend finds attractive—and that's a good thing, avoiding many falling-outs between girlfriends!

♪ SENSATIONAL SEX SECRET

When up close and personal with someone you're interested in, check if the end of their nose is slightly swelling and their cheeks are flushing—definite signs of attraction to you.

How to seduce someone

People make the massive mistake of thinking they have to seduce like their best friend, or the way men's or women's magazines tell them to. Don't buy into that for a minute! *You are unique and the way you attract someone will be unique too.* This is terribly important to absorb as part of your revolutionary new approach to sex.

People use all sorts of tricks and techniques to seduce someone they like. From the bold one-liners that some people throw out in a bar with a scattergun effect, to the overly shy smile one man might flash which has taken him days to build up to. From women who play a discreet game of cat and mouse, appearing hard to get, to those who go up and literally shake their cleavage in a man's face, there are many methods of seduction. You have to find what works for you.

If you're confident with bold one-liners and an assertive approach, then that's what you should use. On the other hand, if you want to slyly catch someone's attention with subtle seduction techniques, you need to go with that method. What I've prepared for you here is a luscious chocolate box of sensational ideas from which you can pick and choose what might work for you. What will make you sensational at seducing the person you're attracted to, is finding what works best for you.

BEFORE-PLAY

It's time to get playful and for me to revolutionize your thinking even further by telling you about "Before-Play." I coined this term a number of years ago after hearing hundreds of people tell me how they simply weren't in the mood when their lover tried to seduce them for one reason or another. This wasn't necessarily because of their lover. Generally the person did not have the time or the inclination to get in the mood. Their lover would show signs of being in the mood and their response was to feel cold or at least cool about foreplay and sex.

I realized that to be receptive to even begin the foreplay you have to have Before-Play and that's the essence of seduction. Before-Play sets the scene and I have loads of sensational tips to get you started when you want to seduce someone new or rekindle seduction with your partner.

Sensational tips for before-play and seduction

SENSATIONAL FLIRTING

Flirting is all about making someone feel good in your company, having established your "comfort zone." A good Flirt knows how to make someone feel special without coming across as sleazy. Flirting can be used with both sexes as simply a way of smoothing the daily grind of social interaction. When it's used in seduction it becomes more focused and slightly more erotic, though.

Compliments—Whether you're flirting with someone you've just met or with an established lover, the key to sensational flirting is making them feel as if you only have eyes for them. They have become your world if only for that moment. You also have to flirt with them in a genuine way. Forget giving compliments you don't mean, as people can see straight through false ones. Instead begin by selecting something you find attractive in them and make a compliment about it. For example, if you're attracted to someone's hair, tell them they have gorgeous hair. It's as simple as that! You don't have to write a Shakespearean sonnet addressing the virtues of their hair. Keep it simple and direct. Finally, say it with a smile and it won't come across as heavy-handed.

Make them laugh—Flirting is about having fun! A good giggle stimulates your brain to produce beta-endorphins, which are opiates that help you relax. If you can see something funny going on around you while you're chatting someone up or have had something funny happen to you that day, then tell them. The more you can make the person laugh, the more beta-endorphins they'll have circulating in their brain, and the more attractive they'll find you because they feel relaxed with you! If you tell a joke that falls flat, then laugh at yourself because that's a very endearing quality.

Men frequently tell me that a woman who can have a good laugh—really throwing back her head and letting go—is very sexy.

Find out more about them—No one is more interesting than the person who's interested in you. If you ask the person you've just met at a friend's party all about them and act interested in them, they'll find you interesting! It's a huge and subtle compliment to have someone wanting to know more about you. The same holds true for your long-term lover. If they walk in at the end of a long day and you grunt a hello to them, that's no way to start a seductive evening. But if they walk in and you ask how they are, what was the highlight of their day, did they run into any problems, etc., they'll feel you're really interested.

Generate a warm feeling—And I'm not talking about getting sexy yet. Most men and women respond to a little seductive warmth, though plenty of us enjoy the "cool, hard-to-get" game, too. Warmth can be generated by moving nearer to the person and closing your personal spaces. It's also about the vocal tone you use—warm and soft rather than harsh and shrill. And you can't beat a warm seductive smile.

Dressing for seduction—I have some fabulous websites and shopping tips for you coming up at the end of the book, where you can get fantastically sexy gear. Let's face it, if you're out trying to pull in something sloppy and not freshly laundered, which doesn't show off your physique to its best, you won't look very seductive. That goes for both men and women. And as a woman, you don't have to go out dressed like a complete harlot to look like you want to seduce someone. Instead opt for a sexy blouse teamed with a more straightforward skirt or pants, or a sexy skirt with a more conservative top. A sexy top and skirt can look HOT.

A seductive feast—When you're trying to seduce someone, there's nothing like some sexy food to help you along. I have loads of sensational information for you on aphrodisiac food in Chapter 10. But here I'd like to point out that it's sometimes not what you eat but how you eat it that can be seductive. You lean over and let your date, or long-term lover, share a hot asparagus spear dripping with butter. Spoon-feed them some delicious and creamy dessert. Enjoy your food, as it's very sexy to share a meal with someone who's quite happy to have a good meal. Men find it a real turn-off when women pick at their food. But a hungry woman gives the subconscious message that she may be hungry in bed too.

How you speak—From my years of work as a radio-show host and having read the research about human attraction I know that soft vocal tones are the sexiest. Even as a man, you should think about slightly lowering your voice and trying to make it richer when you speak. On the whole this is true except, of course, for those who find very assertive people a turn-on and that means they may want them to speak in very direct and assertive tones.

Have a life—You'll be far more likely to be the object of someone's desire to seduce you if you're interesting. You've got to have something to say about life because that also says you'll enjoy it to the full—and that means in bed too. So speak your mind (in soft vocal tones!), let the person you're attracted to know that you have opinions, attitudes, desires and ambitions.

Are they attracted to you?

With 93 percent of communication being non-verbal, body language is very important in working out whether your sensational seduction and flirting techniques are beginning to work.

HERE ARE SOME SIGNS THAT A WOMAN'S INTERESTED IN A MAN:

- She uses "The Bridge," touching his forearm or knee gently with her hand as she makes a point. This draws two people's personal spaces together and shows she wants to exclude the rest of the world and have him all to herself!

- She flicks back her hair in a playful and flirty way that says, "Look at me!" This shows she wants his attention. Or she touches her hair sensually and slowly while listening to him.

- She gently draws her finger from her neck toward her décolletage signalling she wants him to notice her "feminine charms"—her cleavage.

- If she's standing at a bar, gazing in the direction of a man, and she subconsciously places her hand on her hip, she is sending him out a signal of interest.

- She leans in to him when he says something—as if she only has "ears" for him.

- She allows her gaze to linger on his face while he speaks.

- Her body forms "The Twist" giving out a flirty message. This is where her upper body pivots toward him and she pivots her lower body away. It gives a flirty mixed signal that'll arouse his subconscious mind.

- "The Slide"—she'll do this if she is highly attracted to him. She slides her fingers up and down her drink glass slowly. This signal is suggestive of how she'd like to touch him.

- "The Screen" is the body-language gesture which signals that she wants to screen the two of you off from other people. With her shoulders she moves around so as to form a "screen" with her upper body.

- If two people really like each other you'll find body mirroring going on—where their subconscious takes over and they both mirror the other's movements in subtle ways.

HERE ARE SOME SIGNS THAT A MAN'S INTERESTED IN A WOMAN:

- Watch out for him doing "The Bridge," "The Twist," "The Slide" or "The Screen" as above.
- Men will draw a woman's eye-line downward to their hips by looping a finger or thumb in their belt loop. He wants to show off his man-package to her!
- Watch out for that male way of swaggering—"The Saunter"—when he wants to show off his masculinity to a woman.
- When walking side by side he uses "The Bridge," touching either her arm or lower back showing genuine interest.
- Men use lingering looks to assess a woman's potential. They're not completely shallow creatures—as well as assessing her physical attributes they also look at her body language cues. A lingering look is usually used to fine-tune his overall first impression.

Turning the heat up

The most successful seducers are those who have lots of patience and take things slowly. I'm not denying that there's a time and a place for a passionate quickie—those can be incredibly hot! However, on the whole, to seduce someone in a really sensational way it takes time—gorgeous, delicious and wonderful time.

♭ SENSATIONAL SEX SECRET

Since I've mentioned timing, chronobiology, which is the study of our daily biological rhythms, has found that the best time for having sex is 10 p.m. since we are more sensitive to a lover's touch. That said, there are individual differences in when people experience their sexual peaks, so experiment to find yours. And even that will fluctuate.

ROMANTIC TOUCHES

Never underestimate the power of romance in sensational seducing. It puts your lover or potential lover in the mood for more. This directly relates to the principle of Before-Play because many romantic gestures won't lead directly to foreplay and sex but will set the scene for that at some later point.

- ➤ We all lead busy and stressed lives, so occasionally offer to do an extra favor for them.

- Tell them you love them, lust for them, want to screw them! It's easy to take this for granted, thinking the person should "know" that you feel this way.

- Offer to do a little of their personal grooming—trim their hair, tweeze their eyebrows, get their skin glowing with a lovely face scrub.

- Surprise gifts make people feel special. Keep it small but make it thoughtful—and sexy if you want to.

- Do something childish that gets you laughing. Have a little water fight if you're washing up or in the shower. Go and have a swing in the park. You know laughter gets those feel-good chemicals going in your brain.

- Blindfold your lover and then present them with a candle-lit feast or a hot scented bath.

- Why stick to breakfast in bed when it can be lunch or dinner too.

- Tell them when they look hot or sexy. Compliments will get you everywhere.

- Simple chores can become a little pleasure. Offer to help with the dishes but then kiss the back of their neck as you do so.

- Pop into their work and surprise them with some fresh coffee and a gorgeous cream cake that you can share.

- Whisk them into the copier room for a sensational kiss.

- Love notes can work wonders when you leave one for them to find during the day. Make it as sexy or romantic as you want.
- Use a text or e-mail as an excuse to tell them they are on your mind.
- It only takes a tiny little of effort to light candles and put on some mood music for dinner—or for lunch or breakfast in bed!
- Write some love notes randomly in their desk that will be a surprise when they find them.
- Switch off the TV and your cell phones when you're sharing a drink or meal, and concentrate on each other.
- Get their favorite romantic or erotic DVD, light some scented candles and surprise them with a quiet night in.

The great lovers of history such as Casanova used romance in their pursuit of a lover. Any of these little tips or variations of them will make your lover feel that you really care for them.

SOME SENSATIONAL TECHNIQUES TO LAVISH ON A LOVER OR SOON-TO-BE-LOVER!

- Using your hands, feed your lover, taking your time to do things like pluck grapes slowly before pushing them gently between their lips.
- Drip some honey or chocolate sauce on to your own fingers, lick it sensually and then lean over and kiss

them with your sticky lips. Just enough of the lovely, gooey honey or chocolate will be on your lips for them to taste.

- As you touch their hand, run your fingers up inside the sensitive skin of their inner wrist. Then bring their inner wrist to your lips and gently stroke it with your lips and tongue.

- As you hold them tight for a goodnight kiss or cuddle with them on the sofa, run your fingers around their lips and down over their chin and neck. It's not too forward a gesture if you haven't slept with them yet and feels fantastic.

- If they bite into chocolate or suck on a sweet, lean over and kiss them softly on the lips and suck part of the sweetness into your mouth.

- During a kiss or cuddle, nuzzle your nose between the back of their ear and neck, which is a highly sensitive area full of little nerve endings. Circle the tip of your nose around the soft skin to send goose bumps down their body.

- Let your fingertips accidentally brush across their nipples, thighs or stomach.

- Give them a sly smile and whisper to them what you'd like to do to them—make it as raunchy as you think they'd like!

SENSATIONAL KISSING

Kissing is very important to seduction. Not only does the human mouth form the vessel by which we receive our "life blood"—food and water—but we also use it to communicate and make love. Desmond Morris has gone so far as to say that our ancient ancestors probably fed their babies by first chewing the food and then kissing it into the child's mouth. This would provide intense and intimate human bonds.

The human baby uses its mouth to explore and search out its mother's breast or bottle. We also learn to speak with our mouth and as we get older it's used for affectionate kissing. Then as we become young lovers, we get as much pleasure as contentment from our mouths. Using the lips, tongue and mouth in kissing mimics the act of full penetration during making love, so it's highly symbolic and erotic.

☙ SENSATIONAL SEX SECRET

Never underestimate the power of a kiss. Literally hundreds of women have complained to me personally that their man stops kissing them after the main honeymoon phase, except to say goodbye or hello. Studies that research the ups and downs of sexual relationships also confirm this—that women miss the kissing that they get early in a relationship. So keep puckering up whether you've been together one year, ten or twenty years!

KISSING TIPS

Ensure your teeth are clean and your breath is fresh and that the person you're with wants to be kissed.

It's all right if you've both been eating garlicky or spicy food but not if only you have. If you're not near a toothbrush, suck a mint before trying to kiss them (more on the delights of mints and oral sex in Chapter 6).

Start slowly and carefully—no lunging allowed. Men should probably take the lead as one poll found that 56 percent of people think men should initiate kissing, though I think women should too.

A certain amount of wetness is sexy and seductive but make sure you don't get too much saliva into his/her mouth!

Relax and loosen your lips so they don't feel hard to the touch. Only 9 percent of women think that firm pressure makes for the best kissing.

If he/she is enjoying your kiss then keep it going. A long kiss is very erotic.

Take a breather if your mouth gets tired. While you're not kissing you can simply nuzzle their face and neck gently.

Also, try stroking their lips gently with the very tips of your fingers.

**⚲ SENSATIONAL
SEX SECRET**

Thinking about how wet a kiss should or shouldn't be reminds me that during oral sex (loads coming in Chapter 6) use extra saliva to lubricate her vagina or his penis. As long as you know each other's sexual history, this is fine. A man can also suck some of her natural lubrication out, swirl it with some of his saliva in his mouth, then "feed it" drop by drop into her mouth for a really sensational technique!

The kissing techniques here can be used to sensational effect on any part of your lover's body, so experiment! You can also move from ever-so-gentle kissing sensations to much more passionate ones, depending on your mood and what feels good.

Sensational kissing techniques

THE BEGINNER'S KISS

That first kiss with someone is something we never forget. Unfortunately, that first moment can be make or break and turn someone off. So keep it simple and just brush your lips against theirs. Next, try gently pressing your lips against theirs and making a little swirling action in very slow motion. Don't forget your first kiss, or any other kiss, can then roam around their lips on to the soft flesh of their cheeks, chin and under the nose. Sensational with practically no effort!

THE SLIDING KISS

This is the beginners' French Kiss. Slide your tongue gently back and forth, or in and out of their mouth. It's the gentleness that counts while warming up. This kiss is fantastic when you use your tongue to slide food erotically on or off of their body.

THE CLASSIC FRENCH KISS

Adolescents giggle about their first French kiss, which is unsurprising, since it can be all tickly and squirmy if done wrong. Relax your lips and open your mouth about halfway so you're not accused of "eating someone's face off." Your tongue should gently probe around the delicate skin inside the mouth. With more experience you can swirl your tongue.

THE VACUUM KISS

This is a passionate kiss not for beginners. Your lips need to relax and circle around your lover's lips. Use a gentle sucking action to pull on the outer rim of their lips. Then momentarily release the pressure around their lips before reapplying. You may also focus on their upper or lower lip and apply the vacuum action to that. Finally, when used during French kissing on their tongue it feels sensational.

THE MEDIEVAL NECKLET

Imagine a Knight of the Round Table encircling the low-cut neckline of a medieval Lady with gentle kisses. Using a gentle pressure, circle your lover's neck with individual kisses. Start at their earlobe and work your way around their neck back up behind the other ear lobe. Men and women equally enjoy the slow and sensual feeling along their neckline.

THE NAUGHTY DOG

This kiss is ideal for arousing larger erogenous zones like the neck, breasts, abdomen and inner thighs. Your mouth should open loosely and your tongue needs to be relaxed. Now you're ready to "lap" like a dog over your lover's erogenous zones. This kiss feels sensational lapping from the lower breast up to the tip of the nipple—the tip of your tongue should simply flick the nipple at the end of the kiss.

THE LUSH LAP

This is a more defined action than the Naughty Dog but still uses the lapping action. Control your lips and tongue, and keep the lapping motion closer to your lover's skin. Your tongue should be pressed against their erogenous zones using a firm lap. A very erotic kiss to show your lover you know what you're doing.

THE EASTERN SWIRL AND POKE

A personal favorite of mine, this kiss can be used on the lips or your lover's body. Your tongue uses a swirling action followed by a gentle poking movement. This could be around your lover's tongue during a French Kiss, or applied to their erogenous zones.

Keep your lips relaxed and alternate the swirl and poke sensations. Perfect around the nipple or the clitoris as long as she likes the pressure you use.

THE MEDITERRANEAN FLICK

Another cross-cultural kiss! Evidently Mediterranean lovers have a technique for flicking off beads of sweat from a lover's body in hot countries. In the heat of passion flick gently with the tip of your tongue on your lover's lips, cheeks, neck, etc. The perfect kiss for highly sensitive areas like the nipples and unusual areas like around and in the belly button.

THE SNAKE

This is an advanced technique of the Mediterranean Flick. Your tongue can flick and lap, poke and generally imitate the action of the snake's tongue. Use during French Kissing but also anywhere on your lover's body. It creates a sensational feeling if you use the Snake while moving up and down and around the shaft of his penis or her outer labia—more in Chapter 6 on oral pleasure.

THE DROPLET

Use with caution if you're an inexperienced lover. While on top of your lover open your lips slightly allowing a few droplets of saliva to drip gently into their mouth.

THE STRETCH

A rarely explored but sensitive erogenous zone is the roof of the mouth. During French kissing stretch your tongue up to that area and gently rub and tickle it. This kiss can feel incredibly explosive since it's such an unusual sensation.

THE BUTTERFLY KISS

Your eyelashes can create a very sensual sensation when fluttered gently across your lover's lips, eyelids, cheeks, neck, and across the breasts or nipples.

THE LOVER'S PASS

When eating something you can turn into an aphrodisiac, try passing it into your lover's mouth in a sensual way. Perfect for doing with a piece of chocolate, fruit or ice. Holding it between your lips, allow yours to touch their lips. Then with your tongue, push the item into their mouth.

ONCE BITTEN, TWICE AROUSED!

Love-bites are hugely underrated. Done well they're really not an adolescent thing. With a gentle and skillful touch, they feel sensational and don't leave lasting bruises. The trick is not to apply too much pressure and not to hold the pressure for very long in order to avoid bruising. You can skip the neck area altogether and use a gentle love-bite action anywhere on the body, but particularly the abdomen, inner thighs and buttocks. Up the love-biting sensation by alternating with a slight nibbling sensation using your teeth. Be very careful though!

We shouldn't forget the feet and toes. Love biting here can give enormous pleasure and release tension. People assume the feet are only the domain of the foot fetishist and that's simply not true. Relaxing the feet relaxes the whole person, and the more relaxed your lover feels, the better for your seduction. Try moving up and down their feet with little kisses and bites. Always ensure you shower and at least wash their feet before indulging them. More to come on foot-play, in the foreplay chapter.

↓ SENSATIONAL SEX SECRET

Apply the love-bite sucking sensation over the soft flesh of her pubic bone. This will stimulate the deeper layers of the clitoral tissue, which extends under the flesh of her pubic bone and down into the labia.

If you want to successfully seduce a woman, you should know that her skin is roughly twice as sensitive as yours, having twice as many nerve endings as a man's. A woman's skin is also much thinner. Before we get on to the sensational foreplay chapter where you'll be learning lots of sensational touching techniques, make sure your hands aren't covered in calluses. Your nails mustn't be ragged. They should be short and filed, or they'll feel awful on her sensitive skin.

I want you to have SEPs not SEX!

This is a terribly important point and one of my revolutionary concepts, so please open up your mind to this way of thinking. You've just read about all sorts of wonderful little techniques to connect you two intimately and there will be more to come. For example, shampooing your lover's hair gently and massaging their scalp tenderly, offering to paint her nails or simply brushing her hair. Or sensually licking sticky sauce from your fingertips so that the sauce glistens on your lips and you then kiss your lover with your sticky lips. Being playful and tender like this, you stimulate those luscious little nerve endings in their lips. These are the little techniques I call Simple Erotic Pleasures or SEPs.

I highly recommend using SEPs whether you're trying to seduce a new lover, you're in a long-established relationship, or you're dealing with a Sex Symptom of any type. These are part of my revolutionary aim to help you think outside of the usual "box" in terms of your erotic enjoyment.

SEPs can help you stimulate interest in either an old or new lover as well as ensuring you keep all-important physical affection going when you're actually not having sex due to an issue in your life. It's terribly important that when you feel distant from your partner, you re-establish an intimate bond with Simple Erotic Pleasures. In the next chapter you'll be learning how to communicate about difficult or sensitive issues. While doing so you can bridge any emotional and physical distance between you by agreeing to enjoy SEPs.

Letting your lover know that you care about them so much that despite whatever is going on in your life you want to spend a few moments enjoying SEPs can make all the difference to your relationship. SEPs demonstrate that you want to be spontaneous, that you want to turn an everyday ritual like shampooing your hair into something special and shared between you, and that you don't want to lose that crucial point of physical contact, which these can give you.

I hope this chapter has revolutionized the way you view seduction. There's a bigger picture to it, not just a quick one-liner such as, "Do you feel like a quick one, darling?" Included in that big picture is the way your "biology" will speak to you and tell you you're attracted to someone; then, how you can work out through their body language and other clues if they're attracted back. Once you know where you stand with this initial attraction then you can start turning on the charm of seduction. You can flirt with them, make them feel good around you within your comfort zone, and impress them with some sensational kisses and romance. You'll get much further attracting and seducing someone if you think in terms of this whole, big, wonderful and complicated package. On to sensational sex talk!

FOUR

Sensational Sex Talk

I know you're dying to get on to the sensational sex techniques in the coming chapters and I can't blame you. But just as you need to revolutionize your thinking about sex you also need to revolutionize the way you talk about sex. Without good communication, you'll never have sensational sex.

What I'm going to do is highlight for you the golden rules of learning how to talk about sex. These golden rules cover all aspects of communication in the bedroom.

Why does the "c word" scare us off?

You, and your lover, or the person you're interested in, may well be frightened of the all-important "C word." We're scared of communication for two main reasons. One, we don't want to hurt someone's feelings when we ask for something different or want to let them know that something sexual isn't working for us. And two, we also fear someone hurting our feelings and making us feel that we're not the great lover we hope we are. Fear stops us from communicating. The very first thing you need to know about the C word is don't be scared of it. You will be far happier in your sex life and more likely to be a sensational lover if you bite the bullet and start talking about things. It's the way that you do it that counts.

Are you a mind reader?

Another important issue in talking about sex is the fact we assume a lover can read our mind. After all, they love us don't they? They know a great deal about us too! So why shouldn't they be able to guess what we're thinking about our sex life? We also think we can read theirs. This gives us an excuse to actually avoid talking about sex.

Believe me, you can't read your lover's mind at all times and they can't read yours. Of course, when you've been in a relationship with someone, you two may be a better judge of each other's moods, but you can't ever really know what someone's thinking about sex unless you talk about it.

Far too many women, in particular, have told me that they think their lover should "know what I want and what turns me on in bed." No, they simply can't. Their lover before you may have wanted completely different things. Maybe she liked to dress up as a French maid and tickle his penis with a feather duster, which would totally turn you off! Men, on the whole, aren't as guilty of thinking that, for example, "she should know what I want." But they're still reticent to actually say what they're thinking.

Sooner is better than later

The earlier you start to let your lover know what you like and dislike in bed, the better for your relationship. When you're first with someone and overcome by lust, many people are quite happy just to go at it like rabbits. But once that golden honeymoon phase wears off, that's when you need to really start learning how to please someone. Before that, just being with them can be heaven. If you've been talking about your likes and dislikes all along, it's easier to continue doing so.

Have you ever faked it?

Just about the biggest sign of a lack of communication in the bedroom is faking orgasm. A staggering 95 percent of women admit to having faked orgasm at some point and roughly two-thirds of men have faked it too. What is faking it all about? It's about the fact that you haven't felt comfortable asking for what you really want.

Let's get the party started

Every relationship will be unique, so flexibility is key when talking to a lover. The way you communicated with a previous lover may be very different from the way you talk to another one.

The body language of loving communication

With about 93 percent of communication being non-verbal, you can set the scene for enhancing sexual communication using non-verbal methods.

THE EYES HAVE IT

Unless it's a one-night stand, you should be able to make a general assessment from your lover's face as to the sort of mood they're in. The eyes truly are the windows to the soul and that includes your lover's sexual feelings. It also means that you can use a variety of looks to convey how you are feeling. Either the look will give the complete message or it may start a conversation.

What do I mean by the way you look at your lover? If they're caressing you gently and you look at them with lust in your eyes, you communicate that they're touching you in a way that feels good. If you look at them thoughtfully or pensively it may make them think about the way they're touching you. They may try a different touch quite naturally, or they may ask you if you want something different.

SENSATIONAL TOUCHING

It's so easy when you're first attracted to someone to get aroused with a simple touch. They begin to gauge your interest by how often you look at them and how often you reach out to touch them when you're talking. Then they really get the message when you give them a passionate kiss!

You can continue communication through touching throughout your relationship. Use touch to show your lover the way you want be touched. For example, take their finger and suck it, pulsating your lips around it, and then take their finger and circle it around your nipple. They should get the message that that's the sort of pressure you'd like when they suck your nipple.

Keep developing this body language of touch. It's one of the most effective ways to get that touching, sucking, kissing and licking that turns you on. To find out more about what they like, you can signal to them that they should do the same to you. Put your finger in their mouth and let them demonstrate the pressure they like.

You can also use the body language of touch to guide them to where you want to be touched. Perhaps they've been massaging your neck and shoulders, and you'd like them to rub your breasts. You can communicate this by gently sliding their hands down to your breasts. It doesn't have to be like a non-verbal command unless you're playing a little game of S&M or bondage.

Continue this by using your body. If, for example, your lover is giving you oral pleasure and you want a firmer touch then gently push your genitals toward their mouth or move away slightly if they're too firm. They'll get the hint!

SPEAK WITHOUT TALKING

We all have little sex-sounds we use during lovemaking and you can use these to better effect for communication. Those sighs, moans and groans are important signals to let your lover know how much you're enjoying something. The more you want them to do something, the more noise you should make. It's also important to listen carefully to their sex-sounds. Listen and learn, and apply this to what you are doing to them.

♭ SENSATIONAL SEX SECRET

It's fascinating that when it comes to reaching orgasm, everyone makes a distinctive set of sounds that are unique to them. They often make the same noises when building to orgasm in the final flush of lovemaking as they do when the climax hits. Listen carefully and you'll see this is true. Use this knowledge to good effect—in particular, if your lover is going to come too soon, by identifying their sex-sounds you can then sensually ask them to slow down.

SILENCE IS NOT GOLDEN

If your lover happens to be one of those inhibited people who can't utter a peep during lovemaking then gradually encourage them to do so. Tell them it's a turn-on to hear their sex-sounds. Start by asking them just to make some small noises of pleasure when sex feels good to them. You'll soon get them shouting, "Yeah, baby, yeah!" just like Austin Powers!

TIME TO TALK

Sensational sex talk is equally about what you say and how you say it.

There are many things to consider in how you talk to a lover:

- Never use a critical tone of voice.
- Soften and lower your voice.
- Use a confident tone because confidence gives the message that you know you can sort out any issue and that you feel good about your sexual relationship.
- Use a steady and measured pace so that they have more of a chance to listen and understand what you're saying.
- Make sure you have plenty of time to talk, so choose a moment when you're both relaxed. Never raise sex issues when you're arguing about something else!
- If you want to talk about a Sex Symptom or issue affecting the bedroom, then discuss it elsewhere. Otherwise, your bedroom becomes associated with what can be sensitive or difficult conversations in general.

When it comes to what you actually say, consider these points:

- Your lover may be extremely sensitive about what you say and see it as a criticism, so run through in your mind beforehand how it will sound.

- After running it through your mind, try saying it aloud to yourself; that'll give you an idea of the impact of what they hear you say.

- If it's a Sex Symptom or matter of technique you're raising, then start with a "positive." Maybe you love the way your lover kisses your lips but can't stand the way they stroke your hair. You could say something like, "I love it when you kiss me and want to focus on that. When you stroke my hair it distracts me from your gorgeous kissing!"

- If you're raising something you want them to stop, then becoming a sensational lover means that you describe to them something they can substitute for it. For example, you may hate the missionary position that they love but you're happy facing your lover on your sides. What you can do is say, for example, "I love facing you when we make love like in the missionary position, but it feels so much better when we're both lying on our sides facing each other!"

- Such enthusiasm can never be taken as a criticism! Beware though that even if you're trying to encourage something new, it can be taken as a criticism by a ultra-sensitive lover.

- There's nothing wrong with having fun with enticing a lover to sex-periment. Turn it into a playful little of banter where you ask them to guess what's on your mind—

giving them a hint, for example, "It involves the silky sash to my dressing gown and me being your slave."

LET'S TALK DIRTY

Most people enjoy a little game of talking dirty. But if you're with a new lover, be careful you don't offend them. You might think it's sexy to say, "Get down and lick me like a dirty dog!" but they may be incredibly shocked.

Top tips for talking dirty include:

- Ask a new lover if you can talk dirty to them. People like to be asked.
- Start gently and say something more sensual rather than immediately X-rated porn-film speak.
- Don't start with a stream of raunchy comments, instead just throw in an occasional one.
- Said in a sexy voice, you can get away with saying practically anything.
- Keep positive in the content you use. Even if you're talking dirty it doesn't give you the excuse to criticize, unless of course you're practicing S&M and they want to be called a name or spoken to in a critical manner.
- If you're a little shy with dirty talk, practice on your own. Say the words out loud that you'd love to say to a lover but have been too embarrassed to.

- Give your lover a sexy nickname. There's nothing like having a secret nickname that only you two know to create an intimate bond.

WHEN TO TELL IT LIKE IT IS

I've now covered tactful and loving communication about sexual technique, issues and your relationship. How about when someone just doesn't get the message? You may think it's not worth the effort. But that's not necessarily the case. For example, you might be with someone who is loving as a person but who's just clumsy or ineffectual in bed. This is when you've got to tell it like it is.

WHEN THE TALKING GETS TOUGH

In some situations, hints and subtle communication will not be the proper way to deal with a Sex Symptom or issue. Here are some techniques to use to make these more difficult conversations go smoothly:

- Put the ball in their court and find out how your lover feels about the issue, technique or position you want to change, or Sex Symptom you're experiencing. Asking for their view shows you respect what they have to say. They may also tell you an angle you haven't thought of.
- Don't make sweeping generalizations. It may be tempting to accuse your lover of, for example, always wanting to do the same sexual position. It's incredibly rare for someone

to do something a hundred percent of the time. You'll get further if you avoid such generalizations.

- ❦ Raise the issue and ask them if they want to take turns giving points of view. It's easy to get bogged down when one person, who finds things easier to discuss, takes control of the conversation.

- ❦ If your lover makes what you consider an unusual or surprising suggestion, don't thwart it without thinking about it. They may have a point.

- ❦ In any serious discussion try and take the stance that "We're trying to sort this out." That's far more constructive than taking a "you versus me" position.

- ❦ Never hesitate to tell them if they're causing you physical or emotional pain.

- ❦ If you can't talk about having safer sex with a new lover, or even a lover you've had for awhile, then really you shouldn't be in bed with them.

Being able to talk about sex will help you become a sensational lover. It also stops you from having the "sex problem mentality" that goes against my revolutionary approach. And if you're not talking, it can feel like you have a sex problem. But not being able to talk is actually a Sex Symptom of feeling insecure, shy or inhibited about what's troubling you.

Now it's time for some sensational foreplay techniques that I know you're going to love.

FIVE

Sensational Foreplay

I've already described to you my concept of Before-play that sets the scene and tone of your sex life before you've even begun foreplay. Now it's time to liven things up. Foreplay covers a whole range of Sex-play. Think of it as one giant canvas and you can paint freely on it in any way you wish, but the goal is to make someone feel sexy or desirable and let them know that you do. You may build your foreplay over the day, starting the morning with a sexy look and continuing with some sexy phone calls, or you might dive straight in when you meet up, with some passionate kissing and caressing. It can be slow and sensual or vigorous and energetic.

Most people believe that the point of foreplay is to lead to full sex. In my new revolutionary approach to your sex life I'd like you to look at foreplay as something that's sensational for its own sake—that feels good simply while you're doing it and you don't have a care in the world about what comes after; there is no goal like reaching orgasm, but live in the moment and enjoy every aspect of foreplay. This means you need to stop thinking in terms of penetration and orgasm being the ultimate prize and end result. Instead you'll learn to relish the sensations that you and your lover indulge in.

That said, foreplay is ultimately necessary for a woman in helping her reach orgasm. As I've already mentioned, a woman usually needs about twenty to thirty minutes of stimulation to reach climax. But rather than focus on doing a certain amount of foreplay so that she can reach orgasm, you should be focused on simply enjoying the foreplay and letting it lead wherever it goes.

As a sex advisor, I'm frequently telling people that they should become the King or Queen of foreplay because nothing beats someone who is willing to indulge in loads of sensational techniques for the sheer bliss of it, nothing more, nothing less. If you can grasp and commit to this revolutionary approach to fore-play, it will definitely improve your sex life.

Let's get straight into some Sensational tips, tricks and techniques covering your lover's body top to toe!

GIVE THEM SENSATIONAL HEAD!

I'm not talking about oral sex—yet—but washing their hair. Done gently it feels sensational and also creates an intimate bond of touch between you two. Don't forget that gentle caressing releases the emotional-bonding hormone oxytocin. Your partner can either relax in the bath as you kneel beside them and wash their hair, or they can sit in a chair with their head relaxed back over the sink. Make it sensual and comfy. Light a few candles to set the scene and use a lovely smelling shampoo. Begin by gently stroking their hair, and ensuring the water is lovely and warm. Then add the shampoo, swirl it over their scalp, and ask them throughout the head massage/hair washing how it feels. Then they can return the favor and wash your hair—very erotic!

Towel-dry their hair and gently comb it through in a sensual manner. If this doesn't lead to more foreplay, then I'll be surprised. It may be that you start by having a lovely soak in the bath together and then offer to wash their hair. If you're in the bath together then you can run your fingertips from the crown of their head, down the nape of their neck, and right down their body.

UNCOVERING THOSE NEGLECTED EROGENOUS ZONES

Whether you've just washed and dried your lover's hair or are cuddled up on the sofa with them, push their hair aside and kiss and lick the back of their neck. This is a hugely neglected area that is very sensitive to touch. You can also simply breathe gently on this area, as your hot breath will set this sensitive skin tingling. You'll find that the nerve connections from their neck and behind their ears tingle right down into their genitals.

When it comes to your lover's earlobes, try sucking them gently between your lips or flicking them with your tongue. Run your fingers around the rim of their ears while you're kissing their lobes. Breathe gently and never speak louder than a whisper when you're focusing on their ears otherwise it can be painful—not sexy!

Why don't you each draw up a "body map" for the other? On it you both mark your three most favorite and secret erogenous zones that most lovers don't find. Then take turns touching and kissing those areas.

Be creative with your touching in foreplay. It can be as light as a butterfly's wings or powerful and passionate. Listen to your lover's "love sounds" to see if the touch you're using feels good to them, as already said in the previous chapter. Look after your nails and skin, as ragged nails and calloused skin does not feel good on your lover's skin. Practice various types of touch on yourself such as circling your fingertips on the inside of your wrist, gentle massage moves and fluttering your fingers lightly. And don't forget light drumming, stroking and rubbing techniques. By feeling these sensations yourself you'll know how different they are when you use them on your lover.

ℓ SENSATIONAL SEX SECRET

Some people love to feel little pinches and slaps on their skin during foreplay. But just in case your lover is a sensitive soul, ask them if the pressure's too much when touching them this way.

THE POWER OF SUCKING

Don't forget to use different sensations to communicate different levels of desire. After kissing and caressing you may want to take their hand and suck their fingers slowly and sensuously, one at a time. This not only creates a deeper level of sensuality but takes kissing and licking one step further.

TIME TO TALK DIRTY

Sprinkle your foreplay with a little game of "dirty talk" to create a more earthy mood. But, as I mentioned earlier, mind your manners, as some women in particular find dirty talk offensive. For a little extra fun use a commanding tone of voice to ask them to, for example, open their legs further, so you can stroke their inner thighs.

♨ SENSATIONAL SEX SECRET

For some extra-sensational touching, never forget to let your hands roam freely, even if you're in the middle of a passionate kiss. For example, while kissing your lover's neck stroke the cleft of their buttocks, which is a very sensitive area.

ICE CAN BE NICE

Simple pleasures can sometimes produce the most erotic foreplay. If you're sipping an iced drink, take an ice cube between your lips and trace a line around your lover's nipples and down to their navel. These areas respond immediately to the cold. You can then kiss them "better" and warm them up with your lips. Or use your fingertips to move the ice around their body.

Go posh with your ice-play with some ripe strawberries, sliced and then frozen. Once frozen you can circle her lips, neck, nipples, and all the way down her abdomen with them. Licking the luscious melting droplets as you go. To heat your lover up, you can dip strawberry slices in warm chocolate and do the same thing.

♉ SENSATIONAL SEX SECRET

I outlined some sensational kissing techniques in Chapter 3. Try applying the Naughty Dog, with its relaxed lapping technique across your lover's pubic bone region. They'll love this sensation.

BIRDS OF A FEATHER

Use a feather (available from art and craft stores and home-furnishing departments) and massage/aromatherapy oil to bring your lover's skin to life. Drizzle the oil on their breasts or buttocks, or over their stomach or thighs, and then trace a squiggle with the feather through it. Use the tip of the feather to then circle their nipples.

SATIN AND LACE

There's nothing like a good-old '80s-style pair of satin sheets to slip and slide on during foreplay. But if you don't have the sheets, you can still get playful with satin panties. Many women don't like direct touch on their clitoris and labia but instead prefer that you gently rub, touch or fondle them through satin and lace panties. Or take the satin sash from a bathrobe, and move that up and down, and around your lover's genitals. Done gently and sensuously, this is very erotic foreplay.

ATTITUDE WITH FOOD

I'll be discussing aphrodisiacs in detail in Chapter 10 but don't forget just how sensational food-play can be during foreplay. Try feeding each other when you're eating something creamy like chocolate mousse. Spoon out a portion and slip it between your lover's lips then gently lick the spoon clean afterward. Or take that tempting, warm asparagus spear, dripping with olive oil, and feed it to them from between your fingertips. It's easy to get carried away with food—just think of the film *9½ Weeks* with Mickey Rourke and Kim Basinger. Practically any food can become sexy if used with attitude, pleasure and spontaneity.

VICTORIAN PLEASURE I

Since the Victorian attitude toward sexual relations was that it was "dirty," they took particular interest in washing their genitals before and after sex. Not trusting a new lover to be "clean," they'd wash their lover's genitals for them. Why not spoil your lover and turn this Victorian habit into a pleasure and have them lie down while you gently wash them with a warm cloth. Tenderly wash between their thighs and let the warm water trickle down their perineum. Such ritualistic washing is highly arousing!

VICTORIAN PLEASURE II

Another aspect of Victorian sex life was the fact that they enjoyed a peek-a-boo style of eroticism. Voyeurism was practiced in different ways, including peepholes in Oriental screens, which one would look through as their lover undressed. You can indulge your lover's voyeuristic nature by giving them a glimpse of flesh during foreplay. Or allow them to touch only where you uncover yourself, for example unbutton a button and expose your midriff, only allowing them to touch and lick this area. It's all about teasing in this element of foreplay. Another example is, as a woman, to bend over wearing a short skirt and let them catch a glimpse of your bottom as you reach for a drink. Play innocent, as if you had no idea you were showing them the top of your thighs. Fun foreplay like this can be turned into a role play—and there is more on this in the fantasy chapter.

THE "V" MANEUVER

With the discovery of extra clitoral tissue fanning out below the actual clitoris—the Clitoral Arms—ensure you stimulate this whole region, which is especially great for women who don't like direct clitoral touch. What I call the "V" maneuver—or V for victory sign—is perfect for this. Your index and middle fingers should form a V-sign. Slide these fingers on either side of her clitoris and run them up and down over the outer labia. Your fingers should be pointing toward her perineum. This position ensures your fingers stimulate her clitoral "arms."

As you gently move them up and down you will be drawing her clitoral hood lightly up and down which gives her erotic stimulation. You may also circle your fingertips gently while keeping the "V" sign finger position so the whole clitoral area is gently stimulated. Most women will love this because it's so subtle, particularly those with problems getting aroused.

BLIND MAN IN THE BUFF

If you'd like to heighten physical sensations during foreplay, there's no quicker and easier way then to blindfold your lover or yourself. Using a comfortable blindfold (there are plenty you can buy from adult shops or simply improvise with something soft and silky) you free yourself from the sense of sight and you can enjoy physical pleasures more easily. Make sure your lover feels secure when blindfolded. It can be quite daunting for the first time. Equally, if you're being blindfolded, make sure you're comfortable with the lighting, and with the amount of clothing you have on—or off.

THE SWAN TECHNIQUE

A great technique to use on a man is the "Swan." This gives him some initial penile/testicular stimulation after exploring his other erogenous zones. The Swan is formed by your thumb and fingers coming together in the shape of a swan's head. Try clasping his testicles gently between the "beak-like" shape formed by your fingers. Using a gentle circular motion give them a little pull. Next, relax your fingertips and swirl them up his penis and back down around his inner thighs. Then re-apply the Swan as an upward movement, starting at the base of his penis, pulling his foreskin (if he has one) gently up over his glans—the head of his penis.

With a circumcised man, it's preferable to gently flutter your fingertips up and down the shaft of his penis. Next you can clasp the base of his shaft and gently and rhythmically move your hand up and down, pulling upward only if he wants that stimulation. Circumcised men vary tremendously—some have much less sensitivity, which requires more stimulation while others retain their sensitivity.

DOUBLE HANDER

Use the Double Hander on your lover's breasts when she's lying on her back. It's ideal when you're kneeling above her and unbuttoning her shirt; gently scoop either side of her breast between each hand and sensuously move your hands upward to her nipple. Focus on one breast at a time and ask her if she wants you to massage more deeply with the double-handed, scooping movement. If you're giving her a general body massage, you can also use the Double Hander on each buttock when she's lying on her stomach. It's incredibly relaxing and erotic. Use the Double Hander on him when giving him a back massage. Move down to his buttocks and take each one separately with each hand on either side of a buttock and move upward to join your fingertips together.

EROTIC 8

You can use this massage technique on either your male or female lover. They lie on their back while you warm some massage oil in your hands. Kneel astride their thighs and lean forwards, placing both hands just below their neckline and above their breastbone. Start a slow, smooth path with your oiled hands outward and down either side of their ribcage just skimming the edges of their breasts. Then slowly and sensuously draw your hands in to meet at their navel. Pause for a moment before recommencing the outward sweep of the figure "8" down around their outer hips, your hands meeting over their pubis. Gently knead their pubis and even allow your fingers to wander over their genitals before starting the sweeping motion back up to their navel, and onward. Repeat this Erotic 8 movement for as long as you wish. You can also do the Erotic 8 on your lover's back when they're lying on their stomach. Massage around their shoulder blades, then inward meeting at their hips and fanning back outward around their buttocks.

As you do the Erotic 8, bend over them and plant little kisses along the trail that your hands make for extra pleasure.

THAI BODY MASSAGE

The Thai Body Massage gets its name because Thai masseuses would use full-body skin-on-skin contact during a massage with a client to arouse them in the hopes they'd pay for "extras." When naked, the Thai Body Massage involves rubbing your skin over that of your lover's. Skin-on-skin contact is highly arousing and creates a strong bond of intimacy. You might start because you're laying slightly on top of your lover and by rising up on your hands, you can gently move your chest and abdomen over theirs.

Men relish this technique when a woman uses her breasts to glide across their skin. If you have upper-body strength, you can move your abdomen and hips across your lover's body.

As things get hotter, you can turn this into a sensational foreplay technique by massaging each other gently with your naked genitals. Be daring and open your legs, and glide your labia across his stomach and penis. He can also slide his penis against your naked skin.

SWEET AS HONEY

As things get even sexier, lie back and put on a little bit of a show. As a woman, you can dip your finger between your labia and fondle yourself a little for his viewing pleasure. Then move your finger to his lips and gently swirl your moistness around his lips. Finally plant a full lip-on-lip kiss on him so you can both taste your juices.

HIS PRIVATE MOMENTS

It's almost one hundred percent guaranteed that your man masturbates from time to time. Ask him to get in a steamy shower while you perch on the basin. Tell him you'll be so horny if he'll show you how he masturbates in the shower. The shower is a good place as there's no mess or fuss. Also, with a little of the rising steam from the shower, it can spare his blushes if he feels a little shy.

SEXY SELF-PLEASURE

If you haven't tried it, mutual masturbation can sound a little daunting. Done cleverly as part of foreplay, you can actually get incredibly turned on and also learn about what your partner likes in terms of touch. Without even suggesting it you can introduce it into foreplay. Imagine the lights turned down, you're both enjoying caressing each other on the bed and then you gently start touching yourself. Pretend you're lost in the moment—which you should be—and move in a way that lets them see a little of what you're doing.

Next you can place their hand over yours so they may get an idea of the rhythm and pressure you like in touching yourself. Or slide their hand to their own body giving the signal that you'd like them to touch themselves. When you're really comfortable with your lover, you can turn mutual masturbation into a little floorshow.

Don't be inhibited about moving your body against theirs. A little bit of genital "grinding" between two bodies is very erotic. Or rock your genitals against their hip or pelvis. No area needs to be left untouched during foreplay!

↳ SENSATIONAL SEX SECRET

You can stimulate her G spot very subtly by applying gentle, circular pressure with your fingers about four to five inches below her belly button just above her pubic bone. Though the G spot is located inside the front vaginal wall, a few centimeters up inside her vagina, such circular and specific massage can stimulate it from the outside.

PUMP UP THE VOLUME

Research has found that hard rock music actually gets your blood pumping and heart racing. These physiological signals mimic sexual arousal. So before you start foreplay you can raise the temperature of things and increase your heart rate through your choice of music. Mind you, if you're trying to seduce a new lover, you might want to choose a more romantic sound so they'll feel relaxed in your company.

EROTIC WRITING

Put your imagination to work and write an incredibly detailed story for your lover. Let your imagination run wild but keep it within the bounds of reality—the things you two can really do together. Sometimes, when you want to talk dirty but feel a little shy, writing it down is a little little easier than actually saying it.

VOYEURISM FOR TWO

As long as you both feel happy about it, why not visit a high-quality pole-dancing club. Many couples enjoy watching the show and it can put you in the mood for some sensational sex as well as give you ideas for some private dancing at home during foreplay.

HAIR MASSAGE

People forget how sensual their hair can be. Many Asian cultures recognize this because of the long fine hair the women have. Once you've got his shirt or pants off (or both), suggest he relax while you kneel above him and gently tease his skin with your soft hair. Men often respond well to such gentle sensuality. Move your hair down to his genitals and between his thighs. If he has longish hair he can do the same to you.

THE ROMAN BATH FOREPLAY POSITION

This technique is very sensuous and playful. Get into the bath together with one of you seated behind the other. They're the one in charge—the Roman emperor or empress! Sitting behind them, reach around to caress and fondle your lover. You can also trickle warm water down your lover's back while kissing their neck. Alternatively, you can use this when sitting on the floor innocently watching television, with your lover between your legs and their back to you. Use your tongue and lips to gently stimulate behind their ears. As your arms circle around their front, you can caress and touch them. If she's in front, cup and massage her breasts and genitals from behind, and she can wiggle and grind against his crotch. It's another way of generating Sexplay when you're doing something ordinary like sharing a bath or watching television.

LUSCIOUS LIQUIDS

The people who enjoy sensational foreplay are those who don't miss a trick. Imagine you two are sharing a drink, perhaps sipping some champagne—why not trickle a little into your lover's waiting lips? Or take a sip of your cocktail, lean over and kiss them, and trickle a little into their mouth. You could trickle a few droplets down their chest to lick off. And if you're sharing a candle-lit bath and drinks, you don't have to worry about any spilling.

You could get very naughty, lay them back, part their legs and trickle some exotic-tasting drink onto their genitals to be gently lapped off.

LOVELY LUBES

You don't need to save lovely lubricants for full sex. I'll tell you about some sensational ones in Chapter 10, which is on sex toys and potions. Get that lube out during foreplay. Don't forget your good bedroom manners—warm it up between your hands before rubbing into your lover's erogenous zones. As with any touching technique, when using lubricants try swirling with your fingers, tapping and drumming lightly, stroking and gentle pinching.

Men love loads of lube when you're giving them manual stimulation between your hands. Get a little earthy with them, gripping the shaft of his penis with one hand and the head of it with the other. With loads of lube between your two hands experiment with different movements—carefully, mind you. I've got lots of hand techniques coming up for you in the next chapter on oral sex, where both oral and manual stimulation at the same time is sensational.

MORNING GLORY

Definitely one way to explosive evening sex is to tease your lover in the morning without satisfying them. Pet them and stroke them while in bed, rub them down when they get out of the shower, and give them a big passionate kiss as you go out the door. You'll both be begging for it later in the day.

This is a particularly good technique for people who, for example, always have sex in the morning and it's getting a little stale. You can get into a rut with the time of day that you make love as well as the day of the week. Equally, if you always have sex last thing at night why not talk to each other about what you'd like to try in the morning. The rule being, talk but don't touch until you wake up. Something as simple as varying the time of day, or the day of the week, can make all the difference to beginning to break out of the rut.

TEASE THEIR TOES

If you've never received or given a foot-and-toe massage then you're missing out on something that's an enormous stress-buster as well as very erotic. The key is to ensure that your lover feels relaxed and that their feet are clean and scrubbed. Using a lubricant or massage oil, gently caress them with an upward movement from the balls of their feet up to their toes. Ask them what level of pressure they like—too gentle and it may just be ticklish. After using the upward motion toward the tip of their toes you can try gently making circular motions on the bottom of their feet with both of your thumbs. You can then circle the ends of their toes individually.

Don't stop at finger touch, because if your lover is freshly showered (as they should be) trail little kisses down their ankles to the tip of their toes. Turn up the heat by plucking some succulent grapes off of a stalk, place them one at a time between each toe, and then nibble them out slowly.

TAKING OFF YOUR CLOTHES

Some people are incredibly anxious about getting undressed in front of a lover. During foreplay this can make things challenging because they forget about enjoying the foreplay and start worrying about getting their clothes off.

To avoid having any comedy situations develop where you can't get out of a top, or trip taking your pants off, here are a few pointers. Don't rush. There's no rule saying you have to get your clothes off in one fell swoop. Ask if you can help your lover with their zipper or bottoms. Or ask your lover to undo your buttons slowly. Turn it into foreplay, as if you're slowly unravelling a sexy present.

Once you're down to your skimpiest underwear, don't rush to get naked. Explore each other's erogenous zones but keep them partly covered. As a man you can play with her bra strap, flicking it sensuously. Or pull down the front of a bra and kiss her nipples without taking it off completely. Run your finger under the edge of her lacy underwear. As a woman you can also be playful with whatever pants or boxers he is wearing. Enjoy these playful moments, particularly if you're not planning to have full sex.

NAUGHTY NICKNAMES

As you get to know your lover you can start giving each other your own sexy nicknames. You might start gently at first with things like "big boy" and "sexy chick" but then use hornier and raunchier pet names as you get to know each other better.

FIT FOR FOREPLAY

Time and time again, research confirms that the more physically fit you are, the higher your sex drive and the better your orgasms. But you can keep fit in fun ways like going out and dancing or taking an aerobics class. Go to the park and enjoy the swings together or climb up and down an obstacle course. All types of exercise boost those feel-good endorphins, so find what works for the two of you. Or for some sensational sex-ercise buy a workout DVD to use at home and do it together, but dressed in slightly skimpy work-out gear.

Keeping generally flexible is also fantastic for your love life, as you can maneuver into the various positions that you'll find in Chapter 7. Practicing simple stretching and yoga-type exercises daily will enhance your flexibility.

THE ALL-IMPORTANT PC MUSCLE

To enhance your staying power as a man, and your orgasms for both men and women, you should work out your pubococcygeous (PC) muscle every day. The muscle runs from the pubic bone down through the perineum up toward the bottom in both men and women. Identify your PC muscle by squeezing it to stop yourself urinating. To work it out, squeeze it gently for two to three seconds for ten repetitions. Build to twenty repetitions, twice daily, for the rest of your life! You can do these sitting, standing or lying down and no one will know you're doing them. They are marvelous for women after childbirth to recover their pre-birth vaginal strength.

As you gain PC strength, you'll find your orgasms get more powerful for both sexes, and men can use PC muscle strength for lasting longer during penetrative sex. This is because, once they get nearer to climax, if they squeeze it firmly, it'll slow them down so they can continue thrusting. Done two, three, or more times during penetration they can last as long as they want.

To gain real PC muscle strength, a man can try my special "Dr. Pam T-shirt test!" Drape a T-shirt over your erection and move it up and down to gain more erectile strength.

A woman can gain extra PC strength in various ways. She can learn to grasp hold of a vibrator or dildo and pulsate her vaginal muscles around it. She can buy an Oriental Love egg or beads (more in Chapter 10 on sex toys) and learn to walk around holding them in, exercising both her PC and vaginal muscles.

Your foreplay pleasure chest

I'd like you to be prepared for sensational foreplay, so make sure you have the following Sex-play ingredients on hand:

- ❤ Your favorite lubricant and massage oil. If you're using condoms, they should be water-based or condom-friendly lubes so as not to damage the condom. Also be careful of getting oils up inside the vagina as they may cause irritations depending on her sensitivities.

- Your favorite sex toys. More on these in Chapter 10.
- A blindfold made of comfortable material. Having your sense of sight taken away can enhance all your other sensations.
- Personal-grooming items like a hairbrush and comb— can be used on any type of hair!
- Your favorite Erotica to read to each other, or porn you both enjoy.
- Sexy stockings or bondage ties for a little Bondage-play. More on this in Chapter 9.
- Body paints to have fun with on your lover's skin.
- Various implements like a feather or "brush" to enhance the way you touch your lover.
- A rich moisturizing skin cream to rub into your lover's skin before sex—preferably something like cocoa butter or coconut for added sensuality.
- Any sexy surprises for your lover. A silky thong, some surprise stockings, some fun chocolates or "love dice."
- A lovely aromatherapy candle with musk or ylang-ylang scent.
- Dental dams, plastic wrap and condoms for safer sex.
- A box of luxury tissues to wipe up any mess!

◗ Your fridge should contain erotic edibles like ice cream, yogurt, jams, sauces, honey, jelly, etc. Don't forget that sticky things like jelly and honey feel fabulous on the genitals when very gently warmed. But make sure you test the temperature on your inner wrist before smoothing it over your lover's body to lap off.

The items in this pleasure box should help you maximize the enjoyment of foreplay—although you might find you don't use any of the items and still enjoy sensational foreplay. Ultimately, your foreplay may be slow and gentle, or so energetic that it frightens "the Gods," as was said of the Hindu God Shiva who engaged in lively Sex-play with his "consort" Parvati!

A final word on foreplay

Remember my revolutionary approach to sex and get lost in the moment during foreplay. Let your hands, lips, tongue, legs and body wander and withdraw, touch and glide until your lover can't take anymore.

SIX

Sensational Oral Pleasure

You may wonder why I'm devoting a whole chapter to oral sex, but that's because it's sensational when done well. That said, no matter how wonderful it can be, many people have all sorts of fears and anxiety around giving and receiving oral sex. This is because quite frankly it strikes right to the heart of our ability to be physically intimate with someone. It's a deeply personal sex act that both men and women can feel quite inhibited about unless they have either a great deal of trust with their lover, or they're in the heat of the moment and they throw caution to the wind and dive down there.

While both men and women often worry about how to pleasure their lover with oral sex, they also tend to worry that they may not enjoy some aspects of giving oral sex. There are, of course, ways to ensure it's a pleasurable experience—those tips in a moment.

Before I give you my advice so that you can revolutionize your view of oral sex and before I outline a huge number of sensational oral sex techniques, I've got a message for you. I've already mentioned the safer-sex message but I want to stress the importance of safer oral-sex practices, too. Not only can you transmit STIs from penis-to-vagina and vice versa during penetrative sex (as well as penis-to-penis or vagina-to-vagina in gay/lesbian sex) you can also transmit STIs through mouth-to-genital sex.

Many people don't realize that, for example, oral herpes can transmit to the genitals, becoming genital herpes, if someone gives you oral sex and they have oral herpes. You can either use a good-quality plastic wrap over your partner's vagina when you give her oral sex or dental dams that can be purchased from the pharmacy. Ensure you don't accidentally turn the dam or plastic wrap over during your excitement and start giving oral sex through the side that already had contact with her vagina. Also, don't rupture the barrier you're using—condoms or dental dams—with your teeth! The reason why condoms were made with different flavors was so a woman could give head to her partner while he wore a condom, again protecting them both against STI transmission.

Here are my sexy secrets to get you started with sensational oral sex:
- ◆ Make sure you're fresh as a daisy down there. If you've just showered or bathed, great! But don't forget, if you've been running around all day and have met up for drinks then end up in bed, you won't be fresh smelling or tast-

ing. Women in particular who over-wash or douche with shower gels and/or vaginal washes, sometimes end up smelling badly because they change the normal pH balance of their vagina. Do consult your doctor if you end up with any irritation or smell despite being "clean."

- Keep it fun, and shower or bathe together, sensually soaping each other down. A reminder: Don't forget that women in particular have a delicate pH balance in the vagina and you shouldn't use lots of soap or shower gel that she's not used to.

- Taste is a big issue for some men and women. You could smother his penis/her vagina in your favorite chocolate sauce, fruit yogurt or honey-type thing (anything strong flavored that you like the taste of and won't hurt the delicate skin of your lover's genitals) and lick a little little of it off as a compromise. Also, the way a man or woman tastes is affected by what they've eaten. For example, spicy and salty foods are big culprits in altering the flavor of your natural juices.

- Trim your pubic hair so it's easier to keep smelling fresh, and easier for your partner to give you oral sex. They won't be fighting their way through a pubic jungle!

- Get your tongue in shape with some exercise. Open your mouth and flutter it around, whirl it in a circular motion and generally loosen it.

- When you give oral sex you're more than likely to use your hands too. For example, you may grip the shaft of his penis while you suck his glans. Or you may be touching her labia while you lick and tease around her clitoris. Because of this, make sure your nails are filed and your hands are clean.

- Something many women complain about is that their lover wants oral sex but doesn't necessarily want to give it. When it comes to good bedroom manners, if you expect to receive it then you should expect to give oral pleasure back!

- As I outlined in Chapter 4, it's important to talk about your feelings because many people feel anxious about oral sex. A good moment might be when you're enjoying a little foreplay and you kiss them gently around their hips and stomach. Ask them if they want you to go further.

- Once you've asked them if you can give them oral, keep asking what they like during oral sex. Try a few things and ask what feels good and what doesn't.

- A woman may prefer a man to start using his lips only, as her clitoris is sensitive to, for example, little jabs of the tongue. So kiss her genitals as you would if you were kissing her lips.

- Some people might have an issue with allowing their partner to climax in their mouth. Let your lover know that you're happy to give them oral pleasure but will move your mouth when the time comes for them to orgasm. They should give you warning when they've reached that point.

👁 Finally, never feel pressured into giving/receiving oral sex
if it's not your cup of tea. To be fair to your lover, if
they've asked you to give them oral, at least lavish a few
kisses around their genitals while you fondle them and
perhaps bring them to climax with a hand job.

Almost more important than any of the tips I've outlined are your
feelings about and attitudes toward oral sex. Research shows that
more and more couples enjoy oral sex, and this is an important
development. However, many couples haven't accepted the fact
that it's far easier for many women, on the whole, to reach climax
through oral sex. Many women realize this but keep it secret
from their partner. This is because some men have an outdated
attitude that sex means intercourse. But some women also feel
that somehow it's wrong that they prefer oral sex. It's time you
banished this attitude from your mind if that's the way you feel.

You need to revolutionize your definition of what sex is and it
should include anything from sensual enjoyment to having a climax. It's about accepting that however you climax is normal! You
do not have to climax through penetration. You can climax in any
way you wish and that may be through oral sex.

Ask before you give

I keep mentioning the fact that you need to talk to your lover
throughout any Sex-play. And this should continue during oral
sex. Both men and women more often than not like their lover to

start very gently and build the pressure of oral sex as they get more excited. As mentioned, he may start on a woman with little kisses and then build to using his tongue. Or a woman might like her lover to continue using his lips, moving them in a circular, grinding motion. If you don't ask, you won't find out! Women, if you're reaching the point of climax, don't push his head too hard into your vagina. And men, don't suddenly expect her to deep throat. You don't want to hurt your lover's face, mouth or throat by getting carried away with your climax. And you don't want to get speared by their teeth, either.

Getting started

Just as with kissing, there are all sorts of oral techniques you can try using with your lips, tongue and mouth. People assume it's just simply a matter of licking, etc. If this is your attitude toward oral sex, it's time to revolutionize your approach. It really is an art form where you can indulge your lover in the most sensational pleasure. Yes there's room for a little kissing and nibbling if passion overtakes you both and you go for full-on sex. But otherwise it is far more than just getting down there and lapping away. You can really indulge your lover when it comes to oral sex. By altering slightly what you do with your mouth, you can change the sensations greatly.

Take your time and experiment with the following:

LICKING

People wonder how they should use their tongue during oral sex. If you imagine you're licking a lollipop, that's a good place to start. You'd lick it gently, wouldn't you?

For her: You can use licking strokes along her pubic bone and then upward on her outer and inner labia, her introitus (the opening to her vagina), and around her clitoris.

For him: Use licking strokes gently from the base of his shaft up to his glans. You can also gently lick his perineum—the area of skin between his testicles and anus.

LAPPING

Time to imagine you're lapping a luscious ice cream cone! This is a larger version of licking. As with the Naughty Dog Kiss, allow your mouth to go slack and lap with a completely relaxed tongue.

For her: Use these larger lapping actions from her perineum to her introitus, and then over her labia. If she's particularly sensitive, a lapping action across her pubic bone will arouse her clitoral arms.

For him: Once you've got him aroused, you can use lapping strokes around his testicles and again up and down his penis.

POKING

Lovers don't often think of using a gentle poking action. Quite rightly people worry it could go horribly wrong. However, think of the gentle poking movement as if you're poking the tip of your tongue into the creamy center of a chocolate eclair.

For her: Insert your tongue into her vagina as if you were poking a delicate and delicious sponge cake. Try using the poking action along her clitoral arms—from either side of her clitoris downward along her labia. Such sensual poking feels sensational along the perineum and anus—just play safe with the plastic dams or plastic wrap. Whether your partner is male or female you don't want to pick up any of the bacteria from the anus in your mouth or give them anything from your mouth.

For him: Some men like the sensation of a tongue poking gently into their urethra at the tip of their penis. However, ask him first as he may hate it. You can gently poke your tongue along the ridge of his glans.

SWIRLING

If you can imagine a swirling whirlpool, try using your tongue this way.

For her: Swirl your tongue gently around her clitoral area and inside her vagina.

For him: Use a swirling motion with your tongue up all around his glans and also down around his testicles.

SUCKING

A sucking action needs to be applied in the right way. Imagine you were gently sucking a long piece of spaghetti into your mouth. This is the action you want to imitate.

For her: When she's ready, apply this sucking sensation to her clitoris. You can even apply it to her inner labia, sucking for a moment, releasing and then gently moving downward along her labia.

For him: Many women think a man simply wants his penis sucked during oral sex, but you actually need to be careful applying a sucking action to the head of a man's penis as it might feel a little strange or painful to him. Start gently, ensuring he guides you in how much sucking pressure he likes. He may like it if you take one of his testicles in your mouth and suck inward gently.

KISSING

Kissing the genitals is quite loving and affectionate but sensual at the same time. Always start with soft kisses and generally avoid kissing directly on the genitals.

For her: She may like you to tease her with little kisses around her pubic area, down her labia, and on her inner thighs. Relax your lips since that's always more sensual than using a stiff lip. If her clitoris is highly sensitive or if she needs a lot of stimulation to reach climax, try placing your lips very gently around her clitoris and simply pulsate them. Ask her to hold your head and grind herself more firmly against your lips as she builds to climax.

For him: Some men find gentle kissing around their penis and testicles slightly annoying, so try different pressures out with your lips to see what he likes.

RUBBING

Something most people wouldn't think to use is a rubbing action with their lips as opposed to a kissing action. With relaxed lips, rub them back and forth or in circular motions around your lover's genitals.

For her: This rubbing action feels fantastic around a woman's clitoris—as always, starting gently. You can also rub your lips in this way down and around her labia.

For him: Gently rub your very moist lips against the end of his penis. But make sure they're moist to slip and slide across this sensitive area.

FLICKING

Too many porn films show men flicking their tongues quickly across a woman's clitoris and women doing the same to the end of a man's penis. In the real world, this action would be too painful for most.

For her: Using a very gentle flicking motion up and down her labia and perineum will feel sensational.

For him: If he likes a flicking sensation with your tongue, try moving it very quickly. Practice makes perfect, so do those tongue exercises mentioned above!

HUMMING

You may not have a singing voice but you should definitely try humming while you're giving oral sex.

For her: Wrap your lips gently around her labia and hum. The gentle vibrations are sensational.

For him: Try wrapping your lips around his testicles and humming—he'll love the vibrations.

Get into position

The above are some mouth and lip techniques to try during oral sex but now you have to get in position to use them. Many lovers go for the standard oral sex position where, for example, the man lies between a woman's legs to give her oral or she lies across his hips to give him oral. With only a touch of creative thinking there's so much more to try.

The most important consideration in terms of position is that both people need to be comfortable—particularly a man who might have to give his lover up to twenty or thirty minutes of oral pleasure for her to reach climax. It's important that both of you feel free to change position occasionally to stay comfortable, and to let your lover know if for some reason you are uncomfortable. I've known many women who end up with "Blower's Cramp" where their mouth cramps up because they're too embarrassed to tell him they need a little rest.

> ⚓ SENSATIONAL
> SEX SECRET
>
> To get extra cozy while giving or receiving oral sex, use cushions to raise your lover's hips up or to give yourself support.

As long as you're comfortable though, here are some ways to get a little more creative with your position:

FULL ON

This is the classic position for her to receive oral sex. The woman lies back and he lies between her legs. She can either open her legs or wrap one or both of her legs over his shoulders or around his neck. She can use her hands to spread her labia or he can do that for better access to her clitoris and vagina. Both of you may use your hands to open her labia as much as she likes. For the best results, she can hold the back of his head to guide it. This position is great for lip and tongue "action" but some men might find it a little tricky to sustain for long.

HARD TO GET

This is perfect for a woman who's very sensitive to touch. She should try this position where she keeps her thighs together. He lies to the side of her lower legs or supports himself on his elbows either side of her knees, meaning he can lick and kiss around her pubic mound and labia but not have direct access to her clitoris. Once she's aroused, she can if she wishes open up her thighs for more access.

ACROSS THE BRIDGE

She lies with her legs apart but he is sideways across her hips. One of his hands rests on her pubic bone and he uses this to gently pull upward on her lower abdomen. This action exposes her clitoris. He can use his other hand between her legs and finger her. Using his tongue he can gently lick sideways across her clitoris giving her an incredibly erotic sensation.

DOWN UNDER

In this position, the woman lies on her back and he lies turned 180 degrees to her so his legs are up near her head. He rests gently on her abdomen with his head on her pelvic region. He can create entirely new sensations by licking gently downward across her clitoris. This is another option for the extra-sensitive woman. He can use his tongue and reach down further, stroking her labia and even her perineum in Down Under.

RAISING THE FLOWER

This position is for flexible lovers. He kneels between her legs as she lies on her back. She raises her legs to rest on his shoulders with her calves. He brings her hips off the bed and her genitals to his mouth by rising slightly. With one hand wrapped around her waist to steady her, he can use the other hand to fondle her breasts. Raising the Flower is not for the shy woman as she'll definitely give him a full view of her "flower!"

69

Use this position for both of you to get oral sex at the same time. One of you lies on their back and the other lies above, head-to-toe but supported with their hands and knees. This position is highly erotic because you get a good view of the each other's genitals. And you can also give a little extra to your lover with some perineum-play.

LOVER'S KNOT

Imagine the 69 position but with you both lying on your sides. Again, you're head-to-toe and you pleasure each other at the same time. The Lover's Knot is actually more comfortable than the traditional 69, so many couples prefer it. In this position you can both fondle and caress each other while giving oral sex.

WORSHIP THE TRIANGLE

This position works well for a woman with a sensitive clitoris. She lies on her stomach with her pelvis arched slightly upward or she can lie on her side with her legs open. He comes from behind toward the "triangle" that's formed by her thighs and buttocks. This gives him access to kiss the sensitive areas of her lower labia, buttocks, perineum and anus (don't forget safer sex here—use a dental dam or plastic wrap!). Perfect for people who want a more sophisticated oral sex experience.

SITTING PRETTY

For some spontaneous oral sex, imagine she's sitting on the edge of the bed, chair or sofa, which gives him good access if he kneels between her legs. This gives her perfect control over his head that she can clasp between her hands. A woman will love to have her lover literally at her feet in Sitting Pretty. It's a big turn-on, particularly if she likes to be a little dominant. This position can also be used for some creative sex in the kitchen or bathroom. Lift her on to the counter top for easy access.

EASY OVER

Only for the experienced lover. She sits on the back of an arm-chair or sofa and allows her head and upper back to slip down into the seat. This fully exposes her genitals so he can "feast" on her. She needs to be supple and flexible though, but it gives a daring position that can be exhilarating for you both.

STANDING PLEASURE

When she really wants to be dominant, she can stand with legs apart while he kneels below her. By reaching upward, he can hold her buttocks with his hands to control the oral pleasure he gives her. It's a good idea for her to steady herself against a wall or sofa. You can use standing pleasure in the shower. Not only does the water cascading downward feel fantastic on both of you but she'll love the sensations of the water and his tongue action.

REACH THE PEACH

It's a bit of a naughty position, but it allows for sensational oral sex. She kneels above him, so she can be orally stimulated while he lies on his back. She has a lot of control—she can raise herself up and down above him just by moving her knees and thighs. Turn this into a game where you tease and tempt him by keeping yourself just out of reach from his lips. Or he can clasp his arms around her buttocks, holding her tightly once she's ready to reach orgasm.

Direct clitoral stimulation

If your lover likes direct clitoral stimulation (always ask first so you don't hurt her!), try this maneuver. Place your hand flat across her pubic bone and then pull it gently upward toward her chest a centimeter or so. Her clitoral hood (prepuce) will be lifted, exposing her clitoris. Alternatively, if you are sideways as in Across the Bridge, place your thumb and forefinger on either side of her clitoris, on her outer labia, and again shift it upward gently toward her chest, raising the clitoral hood.

Every woman is different but the majority report to me that they don't enjoy direct stimulation, at least until they're very aroused. Make sure she's comfortable and that her clitoral hood stays in place. You may find that when she's aroused and her clitoris is engorged it peeps out from under the hood. For some women who have a larger hood the clitoris never peeps out during arousal.

Touching techniques to use during oral sex

People are very different when it comes to how they like to be touched. When touching during oral sex, this is even more true. This is because there is already a heightened sensitivity when you're receiving oral sex. So even if you've been enjoying loads of manual foreplay, you need to be aware of this when you start giving your lover oral sex.

As mentioned in the foreplay chapter, your fingers can be used in all sorts of ways. It's simply about using my revolutionary approach to enjoying the moment. So if you're kissing, licking and sucking your lover with your lips and tongue, allow your fingers to explore too. Here are some sensational touching techniques. I break this down into tiny actions because simply using one at one time and another during another lovemaking session will enhance your repertoire as a lover.

TWIRLING

Imagine you're twirling a piece of spaghetti between two fingers together; try this action just around the clitoris—NOT on the clitoris! You can do this very gently while you're nuzzling, kissing or licking her clitoris.

STROKING

Using your index and middle fingers, gently stroke her clitoral hood. This is known as "stroking the mouse's nose." You can also use the stroking action on the labia, introitus, perineum and anus. If you do any anal touching, wash your hands before touching her genitals again.

DRUMMING

Some men and women love a light "drumming" sensation across their pubic bone. You can then drum up around the base of his penile shaft or down her clitoral arms and along her labia. The action you want to mimic is that of delicate raindrops across your lover's skin.

RUBBING

This is a smaller, subtle version of "stroking." I'd like you to imagine that you're gently "sanding" something with your index and middle fingers. The movement is a small back and forth one that's very delicate!

CIRCULAR MASSAGE

Using your thumb, index and middle fingers, try applying a circular yet delicate massaging motion. You can use this on his perineum or her labia while giving direct oral sex. It'll increase the blood-flow to these areas enhancing sensation.

Finger positioning

Here are some techniques to try specifically on a woman during oral sex. Always ensure she's well lubricated when trying different finger techniques.

THE V-SIGN

I've already the mentioned the V-sign technique from the previous chapter on foreplay. This is ideal for stimulating her before giving her oral sex.

THE FULL FOUR

Using a cupping position, all four of your fingers can relax down and over her pubic bone. Your fingertips will be touching her introitus. In this position you may do "stroking," "rubbing" or "circular massage" motions. Once she's well lubricated, slip one, two or three fingers into her vagina.

THE BEAK
Bring your fingertips and thumb together forming a "beak" shape. Then turn your hand and palm upward while applying The Beak. Use a gentle circular massage with your "beak" on her introitus and into her vagina as you give her oral pleasure around her clitoris.

LABIAL MASSAGE
Crouching above her as she lies with her legs open, use your fingers and thumbs to gently work your way down one side of her outer labia and up the other. As you pass her clitoris, gently circle it. It's the sort of action you'd use to gently knead delicious bread dough. Your fingers should be well lubricated and always gentle. Don't pull on her labia.

THE HANDFUL
Again, the man kneels above her while she has her legs open. This will truly arouse her. Keep your fingers together and your hands lightly cupped. With a gentle action, alternate moving your left and right hand up and down, starting at her pubic bone, down over her labia and inner thighs. Using gentle but large sweeping motions, your hands should pass each other in opposite directions as they move up and down over her genitals. Since the woman is exposed to your loving touch, this takes a fair amount of trust.

LOVING THE PEARL

Only to be used once she's very aroused—and if she's a woman who likes direct clitoral massage. Your thumb and index finger should rest either side of her clitoris. You can either pull her clitoral hood up or not, whatever she prefers. With small back and forth motions, gently rub her clitoris between your thumb and index finger. Build the pace gradually, asking how it feels.

REAR PLEASURE

If he's a "bottom lover," this is a great position. She bends over the sofa or bed-edge while he kneels and strokes her from behind. He can kiss her buttocks and anal area. As in Worshipping the Triangle, he can also kiss her labia and introitus if she arches her pelvis slightly toward him. He can place his hand opened up as if he's about to shake hands and hold her perineum and labial area. He can gently rock his cupped hand either in a back-and-forth or circular motion.

THE STIR

Put your index and middle fingers together and insert them into her vagina slowly. Once inside make a "stirring" motion with them. With a gentle action, stir them around and around so that you carefully stimulate her vaginal walls. A much-neglected zone!

THE GRIP

Have your thumb and four fingers nearly together, making a C shape. Then insert your thumb into her vagina leaving your four fingers across her clitoral region. Gently rotate your thumb inside her. Or using this as a gentle "grip," ease your hand back and forth gently so that she gets vaginal and clitoral stimulation.

COME ON OVER

If you want to give her some sensational pleasure then while you're giving her oral sex try this technique for stimulating her G Spot. Visualize your index and middle fingers, with palm upward, making a "come on over here" gesture. Inserted this way into her vagina, your fingers should reach her G Spot. This is up inside her vagina, a couple inches on the front (stomach) wall. Use a gentle stroking motion against the G-Spot region as you pleasure her clitoris with your lips and tongue for a double whammy! More on G-Spot stimulation later in Sensational Sex.

PELVIC RUB

When going down on her and generally kissing her pelvic area, try stimulating her pelvic region further. Rub this area gently with a couple of fingers, a few inches below her belly button. Do this for a few minutes while kissing her to help stimulate the whole area.

If you can get her to be a little bit of a show-off, ask if she'll allow you to watch as she touches herself. You get more information about how she likes to be touched this way than practically any other. You can arouse him by touching yourself in front of him and then tasting your very own love juices. Gently tease your clitoris and then dip your finger into your vagina before licking your finger sensuously.

♭ SENSATIONAL
SEX SECRET

Use your nose during oral pleasure. While you use different lip and tongue techniques also do what I call "nose nuzzling." Nuzzle the tip of your nose against her genitals. This creates a real sense of intimacy, heightening her pleasure.

Something extra

It doesn't just take an old story about a rock star and his girlfriend putting a Mars bar where it wasn't intended to go to get people experimenting with putting things inside a woman's vagina for him to then eat out. Undoubtedly, lovers have had a lot of fun along the way putting chocolates and creamy eclairs in their lover's vagina that they've eaten out. However, do exercise caution when playing around with something that wasn't made to be a sex toy. You should be able to make an educated guess about what might make for some good sticky fun. But certain items can be dangerous when used as makeshift sex toys. For example, you should never insert anything made of glass, like a wine bottle, or the end of something that might break off. Have fun, but play carefully when you want to combine oral and manual techniques.

Unfortunately, you can never predict what might break off in your lover's vagina or be covered in germs. You may get other unpleasant side effects from something that seems as innocuous as a bar of soap that potentially can irritate the delicate pH balance of the vagina or rectum causing lots of discomfort. My rule of thumb is that apart from a little innocent chocolate (or other sauces, etc.), you should stick to purpose-built sex toys. Certainly, a vibrator added into some oral sex feels fantastic. In Chapter 10, I've put together an extensive review of sex toys that are much safer than what you may grab at random to insert into your lover.

৳ SENSATIONAL SEX SECRET

If you or your lover are uncomfortable with the more clinical words like penis, vagina or clitoris, give each other little nicknames. For example, her clitoris can become the Love Button and his penis becomes Mr. Chopper. Use these nicknames to help give your lover what they really want. For example she could say something like, "Would Mr. Chopper like to be sucked or licked right now?" Many people are quite happy to use and hear the more vernacular terms such as cock and pussy. Be sure you don't upset your lover by using a nickname or word that offends them for some reason. What seems like a little joke at the time might be offensive.

Extra oral pleasure for him

Seeing as I have outlined many techniques that apply to both men and women followed by some mainly aimed at women, here are a few points to make about oral sex for men. The various tongue and lip techniques, as well as most of the finger techniques above can be used on a man. But here are a few added extras when giving oral pleasure to a man.

Just as a woman loves to be stimulated with his fingers as he gives her oral sex, so too does a man. Work your way down his abdomen with your mouth as your fingers touch him using the various techniques outlined. Even simple strokes to his testicles while tonguing the glans of his penis will add a new dimension to his sensations.

THE FORESKIN

As any woman knows, the clitoral hood should not be abruptly pulled back. Men are the same when they have an intact foreskin; he doesn't want it wrenched back either. As you touch his foreskin ask him if he likes it moved up and down, or pulled back completely and held in place. Ensure you treat his frenulum with care. This is the ligament on the underside of his glans that holds the foreskin in place. It's very sensitive!

HIS SHAFT

Men differ in the type of touch they like on the shaft of their penis. Some will like a woman to hold her hand stationary at the base of the shaft and others will like constant stimulation of their shaft. Yet other men like to be held firmly sometimes and then stroked or tickled and teased at other times.

THE TESTICLES, PERINEUM AND ANAL AREA

Some men worry about asking to be stimulated in these areas. Some think it might make them come across as gay when they're straight. Others worry their lover will think it's simply a step too far. Of course, he should be fresh and clean, and you need to use safer-sex practices if you want to safely lick and kiss his testicles, perineum and anal area. Cover the anal area with plastic wrap or a dental dam to stop transmission of germs if you'd like to orally pleasure him there.

Men who are interested in having these areas stimulated often prefer some sort of simple technique rather than loads of kissing, licking and lapping. Try holding his testicles in your hand while giving him oral sex. You could then alternate between gently pulling and releasing the testicles.

Positions to use

Similar to getting comfortable in positions used for giving oral sex to women, you may want to lie between his legs, or to the sides of them or, as in Across the Bridge, you could lie at right angles to him. Here are a few other suggestions:

WORSHIPPING AT THE ALTAR

Kneel between his legs while he stands. Reach up and hold his hips while you give him oral sex or caress his buttocks if he likes that stimulation. This may lead to a Pearl Necklace where he comes over your neck or face. Obviously only let him do this if it turns you on!

KNEELING POSE

He can kneel over her chest while she lies flat on her back. While she holds his testicles with her hands, he can tilt his penis into her mouth. His thrusting can be controlled by her gripping his buttocks.

PICKING THE PLUMS

He kneels on the bed, resting back on his legs, which leaves his penis and testicles free to play with. She can lie on her stomach and arch up to reach his penis and testicles or she can lie on her back with her head between his thighs. This is a great position to simply suck on his testicles while you masturbate him with your hands.

Oral techniques to try

These relate very closely to the sorts of techniques you can use on women. Don't forget the most important rule is to keep asking him how it's feeling. Try the following:

SUCKING

Pretend his glans is a lollipop and suck it gently. Don't get carried away and apply too much pressure.

LICKING

Lick him from the base of his shaft up toward the glans as if he's an ice cream. Use your saliva to keep him well lubricated. Your tongue should slip up and down his shaft and around his glans easily. You can always use some edible, flavored lubricant on him if you prefer the taste.

FLUTTER

Try imagining a butterfly's wing fluttering and use your tongue like this. Moving up and down his shaft, alternate the fluttering motion with whole, long sucks. It'll feel sensational.

POKING

Ask how he feels first, but many men love to feel the tip of your tongue gently poking in and out of their urethra. Also try a gentle poking action along his perineum, running up and down this area pausing at intervals to apply a little pressure. Most men have one particular spot in this area where pressure feels particularly good.

HOLDING

Try holding his testicles lightly in your mouth while moving your fingers up and down his shaft. Some men love such subtle pleasures and this is a good opportunity to try a little humming, too!

SUCTION

As with women, men like to build the sexual tension as things go on. This means that later in stimulation most men like a suction action with your mouth to bring them to orgasm. Again, check with him as you increase the suction pressure, just in case he's a sensitive man. Slide the whole of his glans into your mouth, forming a suction with your lips. You can also get some tongue action going at this point around his glans. He may also love swirling, kissing, humming, rubbing and lapping sensations.

↳ SENSATIONAL SEX SECRET

Why not suck on a mint or something with citrus in it like a lemon or lime sweet before giving oral sex. You might find your lover enjoys the tingling sensation this adds. Or you can give this feeling by having just brushed your teeth with mint toothpaste.

Sensational hand techniques

You can use a variety of techniques with your hands before, during and after oral sex. As always, one lover may like a firm hold, whereas another might like a softer one. Some men like a teasing sensation where you wrap only your thumb and forefinger around their upper shaft and gently move it up and down. Your hands should be well lubricated either with his own fluids or with an edible lubricant.

THE JUICER

Be careful with this technique because too much pressure will be painful! Hold the base of his shaft with one hand and hold his glans with the other as if you're about to juice an orange. Start rotating one hand back and forth very gently and then add in the other hand too. Ask him to guide you in building up the speed and pressure of this technique.

THE DOUBLE HEADER

Again this is another technique to be careful with, but done correctly it's sensational. Wrap your left thumb and forefinger around the base of his shaft and your right thumb and forefinger above them as you suck, lick, flutter, etc., your tongue over his glans. You can begin by moving them up and down together, then separate your hands, and from mid-shaft move them in opposite directions—the right moving up while the left moves down. Then move them back toward each other and repeat the two variations.

Biting and nibbling

It takes a skilled lover to bite and nibble during oral sex without hurting their partner. You have to be careful of the tender skin of both men's and women's genitals. Some people find nibbling completely erotic and others will find it a turn-off because they fear being hurt. Beware, human bites are full of germs, so don't break the skin! Also, don't try to bite and nibble when you've been drinking or taking drugs, as you're more likely to accidentally hurt them.

A safer area to start is to nibble the skin of the inner thigh, lower abdomen, or buttocks rather then biting the actual genitals. Other sites for little bites include behind the knees, encircling the ankles and the back of the neck. You can always start by giving oral sex to your lover's penis or vagina and then, for example, move away to nibble and pull on the skin around their belly button.

☾ SENSATIONAL SEX SECRET

If you're celebrating something, why not take a big sip of bubbly and then slip his penis into your mouth so he gets a lovely, bubbly sensation tingling all over his sensitive skin.

Issues to consider

REACHING ORGASM

As with penetrative sex, most men reach orgasm through oral sex more quickly than women. This is normally the case unless they've consumed too much alcohol or drugs, if they're feeling anxious or are unwell in any way. So with this in mind, some couples find it works for her to receive oral sex first. Or she's given oral pleasure until she's highly aroused and then they go into a 69 position and climax at a relatively similar time.

SWALLOWING SEMEN

No one should feel they have to swallow just because the man wants it. This is a personal decision and since I've mentioned ways around this then no one should be pressured to do so. There are also safer-sex considerations.

DEEP THROATING

Due to many porn films, some men think that "deep throating" will be the ultimate erotic pleasure. Many women find they can't take it because of their gag reflex. Also, they don't like the sensation that they are being "choked." However if you are into a little sex-perimentation, she needs to be in a position where her throat is in line with her mouth. For example, her head is held back gently or propped up on pillows in this position. This prevents him from feeling that his penis has to bend around into her throat. A big word of warning here: Do not practice with bananas as some women claim to do. If it breaks, it could actually choke you!

FEELING GOOD AND ENJOYING IT

If you've agreed to give your partner oral sex (and presumably they are giving it to you too) then make an effort to appear to enjoy it! There is no worse feeling than someone going down on you and acting like it's a chore. So again, if you get blower's cramp, pause and let it pass before you continue giving oral sex. Or if you stop enjoying it, then do something you will enjoy rather than leaving your lover feeling like you can't stand what you just did.

Particularly where women are concerned, if your lover has been going down on you for a long time and you aren't going to climax this way, don't rain on his parade. You can always say you're now ready for some penetration, which will make him feel good about his oral technique. This way you won't put him off trying in future.

BODY AND FACIAL HAIR

Men with facial hair don't realize how potentially unpleasant this can feel during any sort of kissing, let alone oral sex. Though it may feel soft and silky to you as a man, it may feel extremely uncomfortable on a woman's very delicate genitals! You can check the sensation by rubbing your facial hair on her inner thigh to see how she feels about it.

Women's "shaven-havens" are seen by some men as ideal for oral sex, because it gives them complete access to delicate pleasure zones. Some women also like the man's genitals to be trimmed, especially if he has masses of pubic hair to get through. As with most sexual things, this is a personal choice and preference, so talk about what you both like. If you don't want the hassle of shaving, you can opt for getting waxed, taking off as much pubic hair as you wish. Popular waxes now include The Playboy, which is a full waxing except for a little triangle left just on the pubic mound. The straightforward Brazilian is everything off, but you can also get waxed into shapes like a heart or butterfly on the pubic mound. For the man who doesn't want to be waxed, he can trim or shave some of his pubic hair off.

By running your fingers through your lover's pubic hair before you give them oral sex you get rid of any loose ones. Saves getting them stuck in your teeth or throat!

♪ SENSATIONAL SEX SECRET

Turn grooming pubic hair into a sensual act. Take turns shaving and trimming each other's. Gently stroke your fingers through their hair as you trim them. Tease them a little as you touch them. If shaving, try using hair conditioner with the razor rather than shaving foam. Shaving foam can irritate the sensitive skin down there.

When giving your lover oral sex, if the lighting is bright enough, you'll notice that during sexual arousal the look of the female genitals changes. Of course, everyone expects the man's penis to change with its engorgement and erection. But the female labia also "blush" a deeper red when becoming swollen with the engorgement of blood. The clitoris also expands and rises up from under the clitoral hood. Just before climax, the clitoris retracts again. If you see these changes you'll know you're doing something right.

Now you can enjoy giving and receiving sensational oral sex. Certainly, for women who experience difficulty with orgasm, this can be the key technique to giving her complete pleasure. Lovers who enjoy oral sex also tend to reach deeper levels of intimacy. Next we move on to positions for penetrative sex.

SEVEN

Sensational Sex Positions

It's time to go all the way and take you through some sensational sex positions. Along with every aspect of sex discussed so far, I'd like you to also take on board my revolutionary approach to positions. The very first part of this is that whatever position works for you and your lover should be your position of choice. People assume they should be swinging from chandeliers, leaping off the wardrobe, and generally keeping up with "the Jones's." They feel the pressure to try "this" new position or "that" one. That's not why I'm going to tell you about a whole variety of positions. I do NOT want to put you under pressure. What I'd like is for you to choose what works for you and to have the confidence to experiment with others. There are potential variations on every position and these are key ones I think are worth experimenting with.

There are a couple of things I'd like to run past you before I outline the positions. Having just said that what works for you is a good thing, one of the major complaints I hear from both men and women is that over time, they settle into one or two "tried and tested" positions. That's absolutely fine if both of you are happy that way. But what I find is that people don't ask to try new positions due to inhibitions or fears. Trying new positions seems particularly threatening because it's a lot easier, for example, to try a new hand/touching maneuver or kissing technique than to suggest to your partner to try a whole new position. If you're feeling this way, I think it's a good idea to remind yourself of the tips I gave you in Chapter 4 to improve your communication about your sex life.

One myth about positions I'd like to change is that people get into one position and stay there throughout their lovemaking session. Again, I'd like to raise the point of going with the moment—of letting go and moving in a way that goes with your feelings and needs at that time. And your feelings and needs may change during lovemaking. If you've slipped into one position and have enjoyed that for a time, there's nothing to stop you moving around into other positions during sex. But again, many people complain to me privately that they're worried about moving from one position to another, usually because they don't want to offend their lover. Quite frankly, your lover will probably be excited by the fact that you've started in classic missionary position but then shift upward, shimmy over and move behind them, and go into Spoons.

Another sexual position myth I'd like to explode, and that'll also help revolutionize your lovemaking, is that there's nothing stopping you from having a break in the middle of sex. We have this restrictive and inhibiting belief that once we start penetration we shouldn't stop until we've reached climax. Nothing could be further from the truth! In fact, stopping and resting during your sexual experience can actually heighten your pleasure. I've known couples who stop and pour themselves a glass of wine, or even make a cup of tea and share some finger-foods in the middle of sex. They might share some sexy banter or a loving cuddle or simply lie back and have a few moments to re-energize. People are even embarrassed to stop having sex when they get a leg cramp! I've had individuals tell me in private that they've continued having sex despite being in pain, which is utterly ridiculous. Do, of course, let your partner know that you're simply taking a sex-break.

Taking sex-breaks aside, keeping your movement fluid during sex is something the Taoists in China espouse as part of the whole fluidity of life. They believe that spiritual connection to the universe comes from the interplay of the feminine yin and masculine yang energies. And that sexual and spiritual union of a man and woman promotes harmony within the universe. You may not be a Taoist but their notions of harmonious feeling and movement is certainly appealing.

Another important consideration is that your lover may be worried that a particular position shows some of their body off in a negative light. For example, many women will tell me they don't particularly like Doggy style because it means he can see their bottom. If they have the classic female fear that their "butt looks too big," then despite the fact that Doggy feels fantastic to most women, they may not want to try it. This means you should be in-tune to any hesitation your lover shows about going into a new position. It may be that with some reassurance, loving words and sensual lighting, they'll be very happy to try it.

Another common concern regarding what position to use is the male concern that they don't want be over-stimulated by a position and ejaculate too quickly, thus disappointing their partner. Equally, many men and women don't want to be under-stimulated and take too long to reach climax. A major myth about male sexuality is that they can "climax in any vagina." Technically speaking though, during penetration a man is masturbating against the vaginal walls. Logically then, as people have unique requirements as to what stimulates them to climax, a man needs to find the right position that works for him. The majority of people may not think about this issue for a man but recognize that for women it is more difficult to climax and she needs a position that mimics the way she masturbates—that is, one allowing the right stimulation for her clitoral region that produces the right friction.

Ultimately, different positions suit different lovers depending on their size, shape, and other factors such as flexibility and preference. This means that going with the moment (as I keep trying to impress upon you), being open-minded and considerate can only help in finding the sorts of positions that work for you and your lover.

Condom confidence

As we're looking at full sex now, I want to remind you about safer sex. If you don't know your partner's sexual history, you've got to have the confidence to use condoms. Everyone should have what I call Condom Confidence—that is, the knowledge and ability to insist on using condoms, and using them in a confident way. Here are my top Condom Confidence tips:

- As a man, try out a range of condoms when you're on your own and find which type fits you well. It should be snug enough not to leak but not so tight that it detracts from your pleasure.

- You can experiment with them during masturbation. This will raise your confidence in putting a condom on when with a lover. If you don't practice, you may end up fumbling with a condom and then feeling embarrassed and inexperienced.

  There's nothing wrong with inexperience (as we all start out inexperienced!) but you can kill the moment if you fumble for too long.

- As a woman, in your own time practice putting condoms on, for example, cucumbers or your vibrator. Again, this will help you to help your lover slip one on at the appropriate moment.

- You can make a condom more comfortable for him by putting a drop of condom-friendly lubricant in the tip before he slips it on.
- Don't forget that your nails and teeth can pierce condoms, so handle them with care.
- Practice how you approach using a condom with a new lover. Don't buy any excuses for not using them. Men in particular try things like, "Don't you think I look clean?" The cleanest "looking" person in the world can still have an STI!
- Be ready with a confident reply to the above along the lines of, "I care about both of us and so insist that you wear a condom."
- There shouldn't be an argument in this day and age when STIs are rampant. If there is an argument about it, they aren't a lover for you.
- Keep your condoms with you at all times—it doesn't make you easy, it makes you smart.
- Finally, read the instructions on any new brand of condoms you buy. For example, some are more durable and better for practices like anal sex. You need to check their sell-by dates, etc.

A word to the smaller man

Lots of people have a big hang-up about penis size. Honestly, it's not about what you've got but how you use it. In any event, after a depth of a few inches inside a woman's vagina, she has far less nerve endings. So don't worry if, when erect, you're no more than three or four inches long, since you'll be stimulating the most sensitive part of her vagina and labia anyway. That said, some women enjoy the sensation of thrusting against their cervix (located further up at the top end of the vagina). If she likes deeper penetration, you can always penetrate her first and later on use a sex toy to give her that deeper sensation. This should in no way be a reflection on you.

If you're a man who worries about your size when erect, it's important to choose positions where her vagina naturally tightens up. When describing a position, I'll point out if it's a good one for the slightly less-endowed man to try.

Sensational positions

THE CAT

The Coital Alignment Technique is definitely one to try due to its simplicity and success in facilitating a woman's orgasm. The woman lies on top, facing her lover with her legs inside his. This leg position squeezes the penis fairly tightly, so she should be careful how much additional pressure she uses. She then moves upward an inch or two on his pelvis, so that her clitoris and surrounding region are rubbed by his pubic bone.

The small circular or thrusting movements that are made in the CAT position allow her to mimic the sensations she gets during masturbation. The CAT is ideal as a second or third position when both lovers are aroused. This is because it can help slow a man down so he doesn't reach orgasm too fast and it allows her to concentrate on getting the right stimulation to build to orgasm. Quite frankly, many men like it because it allows him to rest if he's been taking a leading role in other positions. You can take your time and enjoy the slow sensuality of the CAT. He can reach around between her buttocks and upper thighs, and stroke her perineum and labia. This extra stimulation will help bring her to orgasm.

THE REVERSE MISSIONARY

You can move easily between the CAT and the Reverse Missionary as the woman slips her thighs from in-between his to outside his legs. For example, he might be getting too near to climax because of the pressure on his penis from the CAT. By changing to the reverse missionary this takes the pressure off him but she can continue to stimulate her clitoral region.

THE INTERLACE

Another variation on the theme above. She keeps one leg between his legs while moving her other leg outside his legs. The sensations are different yet again because this means her body is slightly angled over his. He can continue to gently stroke her labia and perineum with his fingers for added pleasure. Or he can use a vibrator on her anus and perineum in this position.

THE COURTESAN

She sits on a lowish chair or the end of the bed. He kneels on the floor facing her, in front of her. She raises her legs and wraps them around his lower back. He holds her around her waist and gently thrusts. A good position for a couple to continue kissing and sensuous cuddling.

SEATED EMBRACE

He sits with his legs crossed, and may or may not have his back against the wall or headboard. She eases into his lap and wraps her legs around his back. Both of them can embrace each other. A sensational position for kissing each other during gentle thrusting.

THE CRADLE

In this position she remains on top, lying chest against chest but drawing her legs up underneath her with her knees bent. It's named The Cradle because it's as if she's cradling him with her body. This is great for slow and sensual thrusting and allows lots of touching and kissing. Some women may need to reach under and cradle his buttocks to steady them if his thrusting gets more vigorous. The fact that she ends up with a slightly raised bottom in The Cradle allows him to slip his hand between their pelvises and fondle her clitoral region.

LOVERS' SNAKE

She lies on her back with him lying at her side. He's on his side. She then rests her bent legs over his hips. He uses one arm to reach around and hold the side of her hips. He can penetrate her from this slightly sideways angle. This is a sensational position for them to continue kissing and caressing each other.

LOVERS' SEAT

From any of the above positions, the woman can move into this one since it involves her getting into a "sitting" position on top of him. Unless she's physically fit and uses her thighs to raise her self up and down, the thrusting is more of a slow grind. Perfect for being a little creative because she can alternate raising herself up and down a few times, and then sit and do slower, circular grinds. The Lover's Seat allows the couple deeper intimacy to look each other in the eye. She can gently rub his chest or touch her own breasts, as they'll be in full view for him. This is a great position for him to stroke her breasts.

LOVERS' KNOT

He lies flat on his back with his legs open. She sits between his legs resting back on her arms. Their legs interlace. She controls the thrusting by raising her hips up and down gently. A sensational position for slow and sensuous lovemaking.

THE SPINNER

Rotating from The Lovers Seat she turns sideways. This may seem a little uncomfortable at first with the penis angled inside her. But next she "spins" another 90 degrees ending with her back facing him. From here, she can change the pressure of penetration by varying the way she sits. Leaning forwards with her hands on his ankles decreases the pressure between them. Leaning back, resting her hands at the sides of his chest, increases the pressure. Being in such a flexible position allows them to vary their sensations and this doesn't take a lot of strength from either partner. The man may want to hold her hips to maintain penetration so she doesn't slip off. Placing her feet underneath her (with knees bent), while supporting herself with her hands, she can then raise and lower herself. This variation is known as "Offering the Moon" because of the way her bottom moves up and down (mooning) in full view of the man. If he's a so-called "bottom man," this is perfect for him to enjoy hers.

THE SPOONS

From The Spinner, he can hold her hips and together they slip sideways onto the bed and into The Spoons without him withdrawing his penis. Take your time easing into this new position. The Spoons position is ideal for a slow, sensual and lazy sex session. Or you can slip into it when you've been having more vigorous sex and need to slow down. The man lies on his side, behind his lover with the curve of her back and bottom snuggled into the curve of his stomach and chest. She's also on her side and lifts her upper leg a little to allow him to penetrate. A little movement, for example, usually with her pushing her bottom back and upward a little, will help him enter her. Thrusting may then be gentle or more vigorous depending on their mood.

In The Spoons position it's easy for him to continue foreplay. With his arms wrapped around her he can run his hands up and down her erogenous zones. He can also kiss and gently suck the back of her neck. Such continued foreplay is hugely pleasurable for her. If their hips are angled correctly, his penis may stimulate her G Spot. Without further clitoral stimulation, many women won't reach orgasm in this position, no matter how much they enjoy it. Suggest she gently stimulate her clitoris or clitoral region (whatever she prefers) with her fingers or with a vibrator. She may not have the confidence to do this without you encouraging her to touch herself sensually as you continue thrusting.

LOVERS' EMBRACE

You can easily move into this position from The Spoons as she simply turns around to face him. Continue to lie on your sides facing each other, embracing. She should lift her upper thigh to allow him penetration. To change the pressure on his penis, she can move her leg further up or close it back down on his leg. This will vary the pressure. Alternatively, if you want a lot of friction she may clasp her legs together completely. This added pressure on his penis is particularly good for a man who's on the small side. Allow your hands to wander over each other's backs and buttocks, cupping the other's buttocks so that the pressure of thrusting doesn't push you apart.

THE PILLAR

He kneels on the ground and she slips onto him, facing him. She also kneels over his erection and holds on to his neck. He wraps his arm around her lower back. They can both control gentle thrusting. This position gets its name because if they move up and down together, they almost make a pillar shape when upright.

THE MONKEY

For the experienced lover. Good for both vaginal and anal penetration. He lies on his back and bends his knees to his chest. She gently sits back on to his erection. She rests her arms slightly behind her so that he can hold them. His feet press into her upper back for support. Very erotic for those who enjoy something different.

SPLIT THE WHISKER

Crouching on his knees as the woman lies on her back with one leg resting on his shoulder, Split the Whisker gives him good control. He holds her thighs, hips or knees, in order to keep control and not slip out of her. You can be in bed or on the floor as long as his knees are comfortable for crouching. Men love this position since it gives them a great view of the vulva that gets them very aroused. It's also exciting for the sexually confident woman who wants to show off her body. I wish all women felt this way! He can pull her hips slightly up his thighs, which allows access to the G Spot in some women.

THE PLOWMAN

Similar to Split the Whisker except she removes her leg from his shoulder and bends her knee down so that her heel rests toward her bottom, at the side of his hip. He's still kneeling. He can raise himself up slightly higher, leaning gently against her knee and pull her hips slightly higher up his thighs for deep penetration. If he feels in good control on one arm, he can use the other hand to gently fondle her anal area and perineum.

THE STARFISH

If she brings both knees toward her chest, and her feet rest on either side of his chest or on top of his shoulders, they move into this position from those above. He can vary their sensations by holding her knees and slightly opening or closing them. The Starfish name comes from the fact that she appears to be like a starfish supported by his kneeling posture. This position requires her to be flexible. He needs to be relatively fit to maintain control of the thrusting, as she is stationary in such a position. He can hold her hands or he can lean on his arms on the bed. If he likes to take control over a position, he'll enjoy this one.

By slowing down his thrusting, deepening it or varying the style (straight thrusts to circular, etc.), he can give her amazing sensations. He can, of course, move slowly and sensually and build intimacy with good eye contact in The Starfish.

UNFOLD THE FLOWER

Requiring a little more finesse and flexibility than The Starfish, she opens up from The Starfish by resting the backs of her legs or knees on his shoulders. He continues to kneel, knees apart with her hips between them. For skilled lovers it allows for very deep penetration. For an extra erotic treat, she can wear a silky thong or panties that he slips to the side of her vagina for penetration. He may like the sensation of the underwear pulling against his shaft during thrusting.

THE CROUCHING TIGER

An unusual but satisfying position that's best done on the floor rather then the bed. A great one if you get frisky, for example, on your sofa, since you can easily move onto the floor. He crouches with his knees bent and angles himself over her. She is essentially balanced on her bottom with her legs over his crouching thighs. If she's flexible, she can slip her feet against his chest as in The Starfish. This counter-pressure helps control his position and thrusting. Ideally, he would crouch and she would be lying where he could lean an arm on the sofa. His hands will be supporting him but she can reach between his legs to stroke the base of his penis. This area is quite exposed.

THE SWING

He lies flat on his back with his knees bent at right angles. She sits on his erection, her back toward him, with her hips pressing into his thighs. She leans her hands on to his knees. They can both move together gently and she can start moving more vigorously if she wants to.

THE LOTUS

As the name suggests, The Lotus position allows him to sit. This position allows great intimacy, as you look directly into the other's eyes. Facing each other, they draw their bottoms together as she slips her legs over his. He enters her slowly and moves gently. Active thrusting isn't possible but deep penetration certainly is. To make access and comfort better she sits slightly raised on a couple of cushions, otherwise he may feel his penis is being bent slightly downward during penetration. Rocking gently together and toward each other, they can create wonderful sensations. Holding each other, or running fingertips and lips across each other's shoulders, increases intimacy. Some women may get G-Spot stimulation doing The Lotus.

During the gentle rocking, they can reach around and caress each other's buttocks and anal area for extra pleasure. Another good one for the less well-endowed man.

EASY RIDER

You can slip into the Easy Rider position from The Lotus. He pulls her up on to his lap, so she's sitting astride him. Her feet support some of her weight and they can slip more cushions under her bottom to help support her. This will avoid putting too much downward pressure on his penis. All they need is a gentle rocking motion that will help contain his ejaculatory response. She gets deep penetration in this position. You can also use Easy Rider for lovemaking on a sofa or big easy chair. He gets seated as she gets on him for an easy ride! It's possible for him to nuzzle and kiss her breasts and nipples for extra stimulation.

STAND AND DELIVER

There are many different standing positions. In this one, she stands with her back resting against the wall. Leaning on the wall for support, he enters her. He'll need to bend his knees and angle his hips forward in order to slip into her. If she's taller than he is, then he'll be able to penetrate her without angling inward. This is the perfect opportunity for her to wear sexy high heels while he's barefoot. This leaves his pelvis a little lower then hers, making penetration easier.

THE LIFT

While standing, she uses a chair or stool to balance one foot on while they hold on to each other. This will lift her pelvis slightly and opens her legs allowing easier penetration for him. There's something quite erotic about this position and the fact that it takes little creativity to grab a chair to help the position. Again he needs to use good control and probably hold on to her hips while thrusting so that he doesn't slip out.

THE SLING

This position is interchangeable with The Lift as you can easily move from one to the other. Standing and facing each other, he slings an arm underneath the leg that she's lifted up. This gives him some control while thrusting. Depending on how flexible she is, he can raise or lower his arm to give her maximum comfort. If she's flexible, he can raise her leg high giving him good access during penetration. She holds on to him with one hand and may use her free hand to stroke their genitals.

LOVERS' CLASP

Only for skilled lovers! He stands with his back to a wall as she wraps her legs around his and places her feet against the wall to support her. Holding her buttocks, he rocks back and forth into her. They both need strength for this position. She can vary the position by placing one foot down on the ground. As an alternative, she may stand on both feet, raised on her toes or in high heels and lean into him. For support, he leans back into the wall, lowering his hips in order to achieve penetration.

STRIP SEARCH

Turning her back to her lover, she leans against a wall in this standing position. He enters from behind, either placing his hands against the wall for support or wrapping his arms around her waist and holding her. Again, if she isn't in high heels, he'll need to bend his knees in order to start penetration. He can nuzzle the highly sensitive area at the back of her neck as he gently thrusts. She may stimulate herself by using one hand to fondle her clitoris. G-Spot stimulation is likely in this rear-entry position. Once balanced, he can reach around to fondle her up and down the front of her body.

THE PUPPET

This is a variation of Strip Search, but with the woman edging away from the wall she's leaning on and falling forwards from the waist as if to touch the floor (like a puppet whose strings have been dropped). She may need to be very flexible for this but it allows him fantastic G-Spot access. He should hold her firmly by the hips so she feels well supported. The Puppet is also likely to give deep penetration for the woman who likes to feel his penis having contact with her cervix. He can give her extra erotic stimulation with light slaps or smacks to her buttocks.

THE WHEELBARROW

From The Puppet, you can move into The Wheelbarrow. Here she is still bent at the waist, but depending on how strong he is, he picks up one or both of her legs as she leans on to the floor with her hands. She leans on her forearms. The Wheelbarrow is incredibly erotic, opening up her vulva for him to see. But an important warning is that it does take strength. A couple might only like to stay in position for a few thrusts before moving into another. A few thrusts can be worth it for the man who likes to have a clear view of her genitals.

THE WHEEL

She lies flat on her back. He lies across her hips with his head toward her feet. He places his hands on either side of her lower legs. She can hold onto his bottom. He eases his erection between her upper thighs and depending on his flexibility can penetrate her, too.

STAGING POST

If you're an active couple, this is a good position to try if you've been leaning on the wall but want to end up in bed. It's halfway between Strip Search and Doggy positions. If she's been leaning on the wall, the woman can then lean on the bed or headboard, or kneel on the edge of the mattress. He stays behind her and moves his hips so penetration continues. He can thrust more vigorously with this change of position. If he leans against the bed with his knees, he can also try some "circular" thrusts for real G-Spot pleasure.

GOOD OLD-FASHIONED "DOGGY"

I've always said we should rename this position but everyone knows it as Doggy style. With the man behind, she kneels on all fours either on the mattress or floor. Definitely place pillows under her stomach for comfort and support. This position is fantastic for G-Spot stimulation. As he balances on one hand, he can reach around and stimulate her clitoris with the other, or she can self-stimulate. If you have a headboard, you can maneuver into her leaning on this for a slightly different feel. He also raises up slightly and can even grasp the headboard if he wants to quicken his pace. This can be fantastic for quick passion in the sitting room where she kneels on the floor and leans against the sofa. Doggy is a good position for the man who feels under-endowed. Pulling her hips firmly, tilted upward and toward his thrusting penis, he doesn't need to be large to give her good stimulation. With her being held in place at this angle, it allows him to use very short but sensual strokes for both their pleasure. For extra pleasure he can stroke or slap her buttocks. It'll be a big turn on for her if he whispers how gorgeous her bottom looks.

KNEELING DOG

She kneels on the floor, resting her hands on the sofa or bed edge. He kneels behind her and takes her in Doggy style. He can reach his arms around her to play with her breast, stomach or clitoral region.

THE ROCKING CHAIR

Don't try this if you are not strong! You can move into this from any rear-entry position for variation. Sitting completely back on his knees with his upper body upright and her back to him, she slides her whole pelvis and abdomen back over his thighs. She pushes her buttocks and genitals right into his pelvis. Next she bends her legs so with her calves she grips around his back while he reaches under and around her breasts. All he has to do is rock her gently. As long as they're balanced, this position is a sophisticated one. It's ideal for a woman who likes to feel the man has muscular power and control, because he is in complete control for this one. This is the perfect position for a slow and sensual rocking motion against her clitoral region.

THE RESTING DOG

If either of you gets tired in the Doggy or Rocking Chair positions, you can change into The Resting Dog. Here the woman allows her hands to slip forward so she rests on her chest and her hips come nearer to the bed, to lie flatter. The man can slip down with her and move his legs flat so he's no longer on his knees. He continues penetration from behind while resting on his hands. If she wants, she can reach around between her buttocks and his hips to stroke or hold the base of his penis.

THE STRADDLE

This position is based with him sitting on the edge of the bed while she straddles him, either facing him or sitting with her back to him. Slow and sensual thrusting is fantastic when they're facing each other. If she gets in position with her back to him, she can use the floor to support her feet and control the pace and depth of thrusting. It's easy for him to reach around and use one of his hands to caress her breasts or clitoral region while he supports himself with the other.

THE RIDER

For strong men only! In The Rider, he arches back to the floor, supporting himself with his hands. He may use a padded ottoman (footstool) to support his arch. She balances one foot on the ground by one of his feet, and slips her other leg over his pelvis. Before she mounts his penis she can play with his exposed testicles. His penis is prominently exposed and she starts gentle thrusting movements on it. This is the perfect position for a big passionate gesture and the couple might only want to stay in it for a few thrusts before moving into an easier one. Another variation is where the man becomes the "rider" as she arches over something for support. He stands between her legs and begins penetration while holding on to her hips for support. He can also give her oral pleasure when she's arched backward, before he begins penetration.

EASY OVER

If you're getting passionate, this is great for spontaneity. She takes off her panties and he unzips his pants. She goes to the back of an armchair or sofa and sits on the back of it. He grabs her hands and eases her over slowly so that her head and shoulders come to rest on the seat of the chair/sofa. This way she's arching her back, leaving her hips/pelvis still on the back of the chair. He holds her there and penetrates gently. This position can be maintained for a while if her head and shoulders are well supported with cushions in the seat of the chair. It's great for him to caress her clitoral region during penetration, as it's very exposed.

THE MOUNT

In this variation of the Easy Over she sits on the back of the armchair or sofa but doesn't slip back into it. With her sitting there, he can begin penetration while he holds on to her hips or the back of the chair. With her arms she can reach around and hold or caress his buttocks for added stimulation.

CLASSIC "69"

If you've been doing oral sex "69" style, then you can move into this position. Already top-to-toe, the woman rolls on to her back and then he eases on top of her, supporting himself with his elbow and hands. He gently angles his penis into her to start penetration. You can also move into this position from classic Missionary, with the man gently moving first 90 degrees so that he's sideways on to her and still inside her. Then he turns a further 90 degrees so that he's top-to-toe with his penis still inside her. Go slowly, as either the man or woman might find the angle of the penis uncomfortable in this position. For the man who likes his bottom and anal area fondled this is a sensational position. Potentially she could introduce him to pleasurable feelings he's been too inhibited to explore.

LOVE KNOT

This position requires you to be flexible but is fantastic if you are. The man sits in a chair or securely on the edge of a bed or sofa. She wraps her legs around him, sitting astride him, but twists her upper body so her back faces his chest. She reaches up and behind herself, wrapping her arms around his neck forming a Love Knot. By twisting her body from the waistline she puts unusual pressure on his penis giving some wonderful sensations.

He can hold her arms firmly, giving a sense of Bondage-play. He can also reach around and caress her breasts.

Adding variation

One of the easiest ways to keep your sex life fresh is to consider location, location, location! Not only does changing the positions you use enhance and inspire your sex life, but people forget that the place you make love also affects it. If you repeatedly have sex in the same bed, in the same bedroom, and at the same time each week (!) it becomes an entirely uninspiring rut. But having the foresight and initiative to try different places can make all the difference between your sex life being dull and boring, or continually hot.

Of course, some routine is quite normal in a long-term sexual relationship. However, on occasion it should be spiced up with new ideas, new positions and new places. Many people find routine sex quite comforting, which is wonderful. From the emotional perspective, to know and love your partner so well that sex is an affectionate comfort for you is a very positive thing. But we don't want that comfort to end up equaling complete routine.

It's easy to forget that as humans we absorb things (like the color of our bed sheets and wallpaper, etc.) at a subconscious level. It all becomes a background to us. And if we repeatedly have sex against this same background, in the same way, then the sex simply becomes part of this background too. Dull, dull, dull!

Before I highlight different places to try these positions in, never get so hung up on the position you're trying that you forget to continue Sex-play. While moving in a position, or between positions, allow your hands to wander, your lips to continue kissing, and let your lover know by whispering, talking or shouting how darn good it all feels!

Here are lots of suggestions for sensational places to have sex. It's up to you though to decide how risky these places are and whether or not you might be breaking any laws. Don't write to me if you get into trouble, because different laws of indecency may be applied in different circumstances.

SENSUAL

- Al fresco sex, out of doors under the stars. Just make sure no one can see what you're doing.
- In the bath or shower, with gentle cascades of water rushing across your skin.
- On the floor—preferably one that is carpeted, or you could put down a soft blanket. If you're carried away by lust, you can go for it on the kitchen tiles!
- Wanting a break from your hard schedule? Why not lean against your desk or workstation, the kitchen or dining table, or the bathroom counter? Be spontaneous when the moment takes you.
- Just in from the bar? Take each other against the doorframe, in your front hall.
- Why not check out the local views and park your car somewhere with a romantic one?
- Let the pounding waves at the seaside carry you away. Make love in the dunes at the beach—on a blanket, mind you, as sand can be very annoying sticking to your private parts!

- Taking a country walk, you can lean against a big tree for support and try any of the standing positions listed earlier.
- On the landing or the stairs, against the banister. Just make sure it can support you both.
- Try the changing room at the beach, sports complex, your local gym, etc.

SIZZLING

- Late at night in your vacation hotel, try out the jacuzzi when the other guests aren't around. Remember, however, if you have an active STI, there is a very small chance this could affect others using the water after you, and vice versa.
- After hours you can try your office when you're not going to be caught.
- Getting bored at a party? Why not nip into the bathroom for a quickie without your friends knowing.
- At night you can go in for a different type of swinging on the swings in your local park.
- In a swimming pool, as the buoyancy of the water makes things interesting. Just make sure the condom stays on!
- Why not let the water lap around you as you go for it on a swimming pool air mattress?
- Hitting the shops? Try some fun in your car in a parking garage or in the changing rooms.

- Gazing at the stars from a deckchair at your vacation hotel? Why not see if you can have sex under the stars?
- Cuddle up in a phone booth at night while there are still some of them left around the country.
- Let the waves gently lap at your feet as you indulge at the edges of the surf on a beach.

SENSATIONAL

- Be very daring and try it in your office during office hours. You might try hiding away in the store room or bathroom, or behind your locked office door!
- On a train or in a plane, so long as you are discreet and don't offend anyone. If there's no suitable bathroom to slip into then put a blanket over yourselves and enjoy some sensational Sex-play.
- Press the "close doors" button while in an elevator for a quickie!
- Just had dinner in a lovely little restaurant? Why not pop down a side street for some après-dining sex?
- While your neighbors sit innocently in their garden, why not go for it in your garden shed?
- Slip into the broom closet of a restaurant or hotel.
- On your bike! As in the back of a motorcycle parked safely and securely.

SEIZE THE MOMENT

Don't forget there are lots of activities apart from Before-play and Foreplay that put you in the mood for sex. Research shows that men who love sports can get turned on during an exciting game. Adrenaline's released into their bodies meaning they may get an erection. The same happens when you watch scary films or go on exhilarating rides at a theme park. You both may end up pumped full of adrenalin and in the mood for lust. Also, exercise will keep you in tip-top shape and ready for action. Research shows people who are physically fit and engage in exercise regularly have better sex lives. Partly this is due to their good health and also partly to the release of feel-good endorphins that put them in the mood.

♭ SENSATIONAL SEX SECRET

To get you both thinking creatively, one of you has to choose a new position while the other decides the new location.

There's so much for you to think about and enjoy from this chapter. Even if you only aim to try a new position or place once a month, it'll give you something to look forward to. Be playful about it and if the new position or place doesn't work out then you don't have to try it again. Fear of failure should never put you off being a little inventive.

Don't keep quiet about it if your partner doesn't seem to have picked up on trying new things. Lead the way by your behavior. For example, you can always surprise them by showing up at their office with very little on underneath your coat. Even if you don't have full sex, you can enjoy some sensational Sex-play pretending to be talking seriously with them about something while they feel you up. In fact, many of the places I've outlined are quite risky and just to try a little Sex-play at one of them will be enough to get things hot when you get home for full sex.

EIGHT

Sensational Fantasy Play

When I ask people about their fantasy life, most pause for a moment as if to give the subtle message, "What, me? I have a dirty mind?" Unfortunately, that's what people often feel, that to have sexual fantasies makes you dirty-minded or in some way a pervert. Nothing could be further from the truth. It is only a small percentage of people whose fantasy life wanders into dodgy territory. There's an even smaller percentage whose fantasy life wanders into extremely dangerous territory.

By dodgy, I mean a variety of things. For example, fantasizing about a work colleague when you're already married. That in itself is fine. Ninety-nine percent of people would have to hold their hands up and say they were guilty of fantasizing about another person, for example, a colleague, when they're already in a committed relationship. However, it runs into dodgy territory when someone allows that fantasy to become an obsession. They then end up in bed with the colleague, perhaps starting a full-blown affair. Or you may fantasize about a celebrity and again let that start to overwhelm your waking thoughts. This, in turn, may stop you from actually developing a relationship with someone in your real life. It's rare though for someone's fantasy life to overwhelm the rest of their life.

At the dangerous end, I'm talking about pathological psychological problems where someone harbors extreme and dark fantasies, for example, about rape, or sex with under-age youngsters. If they attempt to act out their fantasies, this is a very dangerous and illegal area. Of course, I must stress such pathological fantasies are very different to those who fantasize, for example, about a colleague and embark on an inappropriate affair. However, it helps me make the point that by far the majority of people have harmless fantasies that remain fantasies. Unfortunately, too many people feel their harmless fantasies are tainted in some way. This is because the majority of us who have a social conscience are aware at some level that there are people who do have a harmful fantasy life.

The first and essential point I'd like to make in light of this is that you have a right to have a varied, active and surprising fantasy life. However, if you ever were to worry that it was crossing over into a problem area, I hope that you would seek appropriate help. Appropriate help can mean different things. For example, if you couldn't stop fantasizing about a colleague and your relationship was threatened then you'd perhaps go for relationship counseling. On the very serious side, if you were to start fantasizing about something illegal and/or dangerous, I hope that you'd immediately seek help from your doctor for referral to appropriate psychological services.

The rest of this chapter will relate only to people whose fantasy life falls within the range that is non-threatening to their own or someone else's well-being. My suggestions and ideas are directed at responsible adults who don't wish to harm themselves or anyone else. These suggestions are not meant in anyway to condone or give permission to anyone who wants to conduct any illegal sexual activity. I hope this is absolutely clear. Now let's get down to the fun of a healthy fantasy life.

One of the reasons people get anxious about their fantasy life is because often they're quite surprised by what pops into their mind. For example, someone who has a fairly routine or even a non-existent sex life may find himself looking at the bank teller in the local branch and wondering if she loves rampant sex. The fantasy continues as he moves forward in the line, with them getting stuck in a bank robbery together. Next, the fantasy has them finding a hidden door that leads to a secret vault where the robbers don't find them. Her skirt rides up exposing luscious thighs and suddenly, with both feeling a heightened sense of risk, they have passionate sex. Yes, believe it or not, people have told me that fantasies have hit them at the most extraordinary or mundane times. They have fantasized about someone or something that's never crossed their mind. And they enjoyed it!

That's the wonderful thing about having an active imagination and fantasy life—you don't need money, you don't need props, you don't even need anyone else. You simply let your mind run wild and conjure up all sorts of erotic images. A healthy fantasy life can have all sorts of benefits:

- You enjoy it for its own sake.
- You escape sexual boredom.
- You dare to share your fantasy with a lover. They then enjoy it too.
- You encourage your lover to share theirs with you—doubling the possibilities for fantasy scenarios.
- When you can't be with your lover, or you're single and enjoying some self-pleasure, your active fantasy life makes this more enjoyable.
- You can "visit" places and be with people you could never be with.
- Fantasy allows you to escape momentarily from a boring situation or the routine of life.
- It can give you fresh ideas that you can actually try out.
- It's free!

With all these benefits, it's important that you affirm to yourself that there's nothing wrong with your fantasy life. It's private to you. And it's up to you if you decide to share it with a lover. Equally, a lover has a right to their fantasy life. And you may never know what your lover actually fantasizes about. But if you decide to share fantasy thoughts, there are a few things to consider if you want some sensational Fantasy-play coming in a moment.

Another point I'd like to raise, which will help you revolutionize your approach to fantasies, is the fact that, as we always say, "men are very visual creatures." And when they see, for example, a woman in a miniskirt, a little cleavage, a sexy image on a billboard or in a magazine then they immediately start fantasizing. However, the one thing that I've also always said as a sex expert is that women are visual creatures too. And this fact is from sexology research that shows when women are presented with so-called sexy images they immediately get blood engorgement and lubrication to their vagina. So don't be surprised that the woman in your life has a very rich fantasy life. And those fantasies may often spring from what she's just seen that she finds arousing.

Mind your manners!

People forget their manners when it comes to sharing their secret fantasy life. No one wants to offend a lover on purpose but people often fail to consider certain aspects of sharing private sexual thoughts. If you want it to be successful and an erotic experience, then there is some basic bedroom etiquette you need to follow.

When you decide to share a fantasy with your lover, remember these guidelines:

- Think about your timing. If they've just confessed undying love for you and have made fantastic attempts to generate a romantic atmosphere, maybe it's not the right time to tell them about your fantasy to have rampant sex with a stranger on a speeding train.

- Once you've decided it's the right moment to share some hot fantasy talk, then sound them out. As you lie there cuddling them, whisper something sensual like, "You're so beautiful. I often fantasize that I'm an artist and you've arrived as my new model. You're not supposed to pose naked but I slowly seduce you into undressing." This makes your fantasy sound alluring and not threatening. You never want your lover to feel threatened that they can't compete with your fantasy.

- Ask them if they'd like to tell you about their secret fantasy life. You need to judge your lover's preference. They may prefer you starting the fantasy chat, as above. However, you know your lover best and they might actually prefer being given the chance to tell you what they fantasize about.

- When it comes to outlining your fantasy, begin by putting your lover slap bang in the middle of it—unless it's somewhere they wouldn't logically appear, such as in a crowded bar where you lap dance the clientele. However, particularly if your fantasy includes others, you should try to incorporate your lover. Consider how potentially hurtful it might be if you told your lover you fantasize about having a threesome but you haven't included them as part of that threesome. It's plain common sense.

- Variety is the spice of life, so vary the fantasy scenarios you tell them about. If you repeatedly describe the same scenario, for example, that you are watching your lover have sex with their boss, they may rightly feel threatened by this. They may think you can only get turned on by the idea of watching them have sex with an authority figure.

- Honesty is the right policy, but temper this with tact when it comes to sharing your fantasies. Complete honesty, for example about fantasizing about your next-door neighbor might be hurtful. However, if you turn it around and say you fantasize that your neighbor fantasizes about the two of you in bed, that's not particularly hurtful. Another classic example is for you to tell your girlfriend that you fantasize about her sister. Sisters should definitely be kept out of fantasies!

- Even if they want you to "go first," always ask to hear their fantasies. If one of you is more dominant in the relationship or has a more active imagination, it's easy to dominate the fantasy chat too.

- What one person thinks of as a fantasy, another thinks of as a nightmare! Use common sense with your lover. If you fantasize about, for example, "golden showers" but you know this sexual practice would disgust them, then keep it to yourself. Find a fantasy arena that turns you both on to make sharing it an erotic event. Fantasy chat should never be about turning one of you off.

- Some fantasies should never be turned into reality! You may act out ones in your sex life that are fun, and leave others in your mind.

- Sometimes fantasies can be a no-go zone. Unfortunately, even if you are incredibly tactful you may find yourself with a lover who simply will not discuss fantasies. This may be due to them having sexual inhibitions. If you're with them long-term, that may change as they gain their sexual confidence. However, you can't count on that and you should never force the issue. While respecting their feelings, I wouldn't rule out occasionally dropping a gentle mention of a fantasy. It wouldn't hurt to say something like, "I have fantasized about you wearing old-fashioned stockings and a corset." Hopefully they'll open up to the idea of sharing fantasies, even if very gentle ones.

What crosses your mind?

There have been all sorts of research and surveys conducted into our deeper fantasy lives. Although the detail varies from individual to individual, when people share their fantasies in confidence, many common themes emerge. These themes include things like power, control, surprise, danger, stranger sex, exhibitionism and forbidden fruit. Since there is such a rich variety of possible fantasies, I'm going to outline for you the main ones that have emerged from research and from the anecdotal evidence I've collected in my years a sex expert, life coach and psychologist.

A couple of things to bear in mind are that you'll know from your own personal fantasy life that one day you may think about doing something exhibitionist and the next day you may think about being dominated by someone else. Fantasies change! This shouldn't be surprising, having already pointed out that the brain is your biggest sex organ and fantasies are generated there. Another point to make (while keeping in mind my earlier mention of dangerous fantasies), is that even someone who's not about to do anything dangerous might occasionally fantasize about something like, for example, extreme sado-masochism. This doesn't mean they want someone to strap them to a table and beat them black and blue. It's important to be able to acknowledge the fantasy element that allows us to explore in our imagination things we might never do in our actual life. To reiterate, some of the fantasy themes I'll outline here should not be misconstrued in any way as permission to harm another person.

FEMALE FANTASY THEMES

- Having carefree, uninhibited sex—Yes, many women fantasize about letting go of their inhibitions and actually throwing themselves into sex. This fantasy doesn't necessarily have a theme apart from doing exactly what they want and not worrying how they look!

- Group sex—Some of the most surprising, seemingly unadventurous people fantasize about group sex. This theme is all about abandoning caution and reveling in as many sexual encounters as possible.

- Lesbian/bi-sexual fantasies—Many women enjoy same-sex fantasy scenarios. Often these fantasies revolve around how very different it would be to experience a woman's body and gentle touch compared to a man's.

- Sex with a stranger—This theme involves playing around with a bit of no-strings sex. This is a popular theme probably because society still treats such encounters as a "no-go" area for women.

- Exhibitionism—Since many women still feel quite sexually inhibited, these themes allow them a little bit of release from those feelings. For example, a common exhibitionist theme is playing the role of stripper or lap-dancer—being in control of men by making them sexually aroused.

- Sex with a repair or delivery man, your doctor, or anyone providing such services to you—This theme plays on our many common notions about the sexiness of men who work with their hands or who look after our needs. A common scenario is being a damsel-in-distress who calls a plumber. He turns out to be a gorgeous hunk and you have brazen sex on the kitchen floor.

- Forbidden sex with a friend's partner, a sister's boyfriend, etc.—There are all sorts of fantasy themes around forbidden fruit. These allow us to behave in a way that would never be socially acceptable.

- Exotic sex—Being swept off to a foreign country against your will and being kept as a captive sex slave. Another fantasy theme that frees many women from sexual inhibitions. Because themes revolve around being taken against your will, at one level a woman feels it's not really her choice. It also frees us from having to be responsible for being good at sex.

- Sex with famous people—For sheer blissful escapism, many women enjoy the thought of sleeping with their favorite celebrity. Many women elaborate on this theme and make themselves the object of their favorite celebrity's desire.

- Forced to strip—This common theme is popular with women who are inhibited about their bodies. Again, by being forced to show off their body, this frees them from all responsibility for this behavior.

- Being secretly watched/spied upon—A fantasy theme common to many women is that they're so sexy someone has to spy on them. This plays into women's feelings that they want to be sexy and desirable.

- Lady of the manor and the stable lad—Dominant and submissive women both enjoy having a dominant role as a sexual fantasy theme. Not only does it allow submissive women to do a little role-reversal, but it allows already dominant women to feel better about playing this role. Then add to this fantasy the fact that the woman is having rampant sex with someone who's a "little rough" and it only fuels the secret desires of many women to be ravished by rough hands.

- Directing sexual activity with a novice or from a position of authority—Quite risky territory is covered in this theme. For example, if a woman fantasizes she's the schoolmistress and he's the 18-year-old virgin, it allows her to venture into taboo territory.

- Being taken forcibly or being forced by a lover to do a new and forbidden sexual practice—Playing out strictly taboo themes like being forced into sexual acts "against the will" allows women to play out completely different roles. This does not, in any circumstances, mean she actually wants to be taken forcibly.

- The "Casting Couch"—A popular fantasy theme with many women is of having to give sexual favors in return for getting a perk, like a job. Mixing a "work" scenario with sexual activity plays out the theme of power in workplace relationships.

- Domination and bondage, discipline and sado-masochism—Again, experiencing the taboos of domination, etc., through the safety of our fantasy life can be extremely erotic. Think of the powerful erotic tension in the film *The Piano* and you'll understand how this handing over of power can become the stuff of fantasies. In that movie, the sexual demands that Harvey Keitel's character made of Holly Hunter's mute pianist character were exciting on many levels. Did it arouse her? Did it arouse him? Or was it just about power? Her character ended up responding to him passionately.

- Starring in a porn film—Many women wonder what it would be like to star in a porn film. This fantasy theme covers many levels, including wanting to be desired by everyone who watches the film, to being very practiced and experienced at sex. The raunchiness of this fantasy also allows women freedom from feeling that sex is often too predictable and "clean."

- High-risk sex where there's a chance of discovery— Taking a risk is a popular theme because quite frankly, many don't take risks in their sex lives. Joining the "mile-high club," having sex in the office behind the stationery cupboard, or in the bathroom in a bar, etc.—all explore the thrill of sex where someone may catch you out. Getting caught adds another layer to the fantasy!

MALE FANTASY THEMES

There are many themes common to male and female fantasies. However, one very common repeating theme for men is that they tend to go more frequently into dangerous territory with their fantasies.

- Lazy sex—Quite frankly a general theme running through many male fantasies is one where they don't have to do anything while their lover pleasures them. This may reflect the fact that men feel under pressure to find every point from A–Z on their lover's body and to pleasure them in every way possible!

- Voyeuristic fantasies—Most men will admit to having had some sort of voyeuristic fantasy. Perhaps watching their neighbor strip off and get into her shower. Or watching another couple make love. This may explain the popularity of so-called "dogging" activity. This is where people seek out other like-minded people to have sex in front of, or with, usually parked up in a fairly secluded setting.

- Sex with forbidden people like nuns, nannies and school teachers—Whereas women quite commonly fantasize about forbidden figures like school masters or being forbidden figures like school mistresses, men often take this further, fantasizing about ultimate forbidden figures such as nuns.

- Sex with prostitutes—Even men who'd never consider using a prostitute fantasize about paid-for sex. Not only does it cross into the territory of rather dirty sex, it also means that they can take their wallet out and pay for exactly what they want. There's so much pressure on men to perform today that many of these fantasies reflect a simple desire for uncomplicated sex without strings.

- Ravishing an unlikely lover—Women are often surprised by the fact their lover fantasizes about, for example, taking the mouse-like librarian. But this plays into the theme of being irresistible even to women who shouldn't want them. Such a theme proves to them they can seduce anyone.

- Being seduced by someone forbidden in your personal life—Seducing a girlfriend's mother, your wife's best friend, etc., is a theme that continues the forbidden fruit theme. Playing very close to home like this is truly forbidden and, like women, men relish the idea of doing something dirty on their own doorsteps.

- Watching lesbian sex—Ninety-nine percent of straight men admit to fantasizing about two women making love together. There are many levels on which they find this a turn-on. Often they say they're amazed by the gentleness of two women making love. They also believe it'll reveal all sorts of secrets about women. Their fantasy usually ends with them being invited to join in the action!

- Bondage, domination and sadomasochism—Men are often more open about their curiosity for BDSM. Many men want to take a more submissive role and be dominated by the partner in their fantasies. Other men get off on being the dominant partner. Many look forward to playing out different power roles in fantasy Sex-play.

- Group and three-way sex—Men often have a more free and easy fantasy view of group sex. They are often better at distinguishing the purely physical aspects of having sex with a lot of different people. Many women express guilt over such fantasies. Another difference is that women love the idea of the sensuality of experiencing many different bodies at once whereas men's fantasies often revolve around proving their masculinity in front of a crowd.

- Being a successful businessman—Many men fantasize about abusing the power of their position. They fantasize about being the boss who can have any secretary he wants. They also fantasize about risky sex around the copy machine, in the staff bathroom, etc.

- Being seduced by a sexy nurse—This is a typical fantasy appealing to the side of a man's nature that longs to be looked after and nurtured. Of course this nurturing involves raunchy sex!

- Watching his lover being taken by another man—This voyeuristic fantasy theme is more common in men than women. Many men are aroused by the idea of watching another man take their lover. For many it's about the competition involved where their fantasy continues down the path where she says that he's better than the stranger she's just had sex with.

- Gay sex encounter—Less frequently men will openly admit to having gay sex fantasies. In confidence many do admit to this out of curiosity.

- Being "feminized"—Some women are shocked by a man who fantasizes about being feminized. However, when placed in the context that they simply want to give up a dominant, social role they may hold, it's easier to understand. By far the majority of men who have this fantasy do not want to actually change their sex or become cross-dressers.

- Having really dirty/raunchy sex with someone who is rough or "unwashed"—Appealing to the very basic and raunchy side of their nature, many men fantasize about picking up a really rough woman and having rampant sex with her.

- Having sex with a pregnant woman—The idea of a pregnant woman with ripe breasts and a lush stomach arouses many men. Fantasies about pregnant women are quite common and often involve the gentler side of a man's nature.

- Seducing a stranger on a train, plane, etc.—At the heart of such a fantasy is being irresistible to a stranger. These fantasies can boost the ego of men who often secretly worry about their desirability. The no-strings aspect appeals to men who sometimes feel overwhelmed or threatened by requests for extra foreplay, etc.

- Being a police/prison officer that takes a beautiful prisoner—The basis of this fantasy is about control. It's also about abuse of their position and taking advantage of someone who doesn't have a choice.

- Anal sex—With many women completely uninterested in anal sex, this is still a little of a taboo. Anything that's taboo is like showing red to a bull.

- Being the sexiest super-stud in the world—The theme of proving themselves as great lovers recurs in many fantasies. Although women would find this quite juvenile and an uninteresting fantasy, for a man it's a way of boosting their ego.

- Seducing a younger woman—Taking the pressure off his lovemaking skills by making himself an older man in a fantasy, he feels he can do what he wants with a younger lover. Often these fantasies involve her doing as he instructs. Bolstering the male ego, these fantasies also include her seeing him as a master of sex.

- Seducing a gorgeous film star or pin-up—Equal with women, men spend a lot of time fantasizing about their favorite film and pop stars. It's completely about stroking their ego and enjoying the ultimate fantasy with a gorgeous woman who wants them.

- Directing or starring in a porn film—Any which way you look at it, many men enjoy porn film fantasies. Taking either the directorial role and telling porn stars what to do, or being the porn stars themselves. Many men love the idea of the completely sexualized environment of a porn-film set, which provides them with lots of fantasy ideas.

Sensational role play

People often assume that by sharing their fantasies, I automatically mean they will have to do role play. Many people find that quite threatening and understandably so. Nothing could be further from the truth, as many, many people successfully share their secret sexual fantasies while simply caressing and making love to each other.

However, if you're interested in taking it a step further, there are many positive reasons to do so. For starters, role playing a fantasy can be very releasing for a couple. It means that instead of being themselves and feeling inhibited about a sexual experience they can "pretend" to be someone else and shed their inhibitions. After all, they reason that if they're pretending to be someone else then it's not their "real self" they are putting on the line. This can be very positive and enhancing for a sexual relationship.

Just as sharing your fantasies can keep your love life exciting, so too can role play. It gives you a whole new way of relating to each other sexually. Really, anything goes and you can continually dream up new role plays to try. Or you can re-use the ones you find terribly exciting. There are no rules!

RULES OF ROLE PLAY

Having just said there are no rules, in fact there are some rules of etiquette. Let me outline these so that you can have a sensational experience:

- It's best to start talking about a fantasy before you even try a role play. And before you talk about fantasy you'll have already read above how to introduce a fantasy to your lover without upsetting them.
- Just in case the role play doesn't work out, it's best to keep costumes and other such items to a minimum. I would hate for you to go out and spend a fortune on some dramatic costumes and accessories and find out you didn't enjoy the role play experience.

- Never force a lover to engage in a role play that turns them off. This will backfire on you.
- Ensure that wherever you play out a role play you don't land yourselves in trouble with the law in any way.
- Don't use items to accessorize your role play that actually could be dangerous—like glass bottles inserted into the vagina, etc., when you're pretending to be a vineyard owner.
- If you enjoy role play, be careful how much you spend. Some costumes made of PVC, etc., can cost hundreds of dollars. If you have any money worries, you can role play without cost. You simply "act" as actors would do.
- Just as anything potentially can become an obsession, don't allow role play to take over your sex life. Some couples I've met have become so obsessed with a role play that they never end up having simple, loving sex. Ultimately one or the other starts to feel that they're not really in touch with each other anymore.

GETTING STARTED

After you've had a sexy chat with your lover about what role play you'd like to try, see what you've already got in your bedroom that might add to the experience. You might decide to visit a costume shop and rent something, because costume parties are so popular there are loads of costumes to choose from. Many adult sex shops have adult role play outfits available. From the non-surprising French Maid outfit to much more exotic items, there's lots to choose from. Internet sites also carry an array of interesting gear.

To get you started, here are a few examples of fantasies that translate easily into role plays. None of these require costumes, unless you want to go to those lengths. These are only suggestions based on what people tell me have worked well for them.

NAUGHTY NEIGHBOR

One of the simplest role plays is to pretend you're the next-door neighbor who has come over to borrow something—but you're not an ordinary neighbor, you're a dirty-flirty neighbor! No costumes necessary, but just a little of imagination when it comes to playing a cat-and-mouse game of flirting with each other.

STRANGERS IN THE NIGHT

This is a very good fantasy to turn into a role play that is fantastic for boosting your sex life. What you need to do is agree in advance what your new names are going to be and where to meet. Choose a bar or club you don't know, so you aren't interrupted by any regulars or friends. Once you spot each other, pretend you're strangers and start flirting. You can take this role play any place in your imagination you want. You could make it even more risqué and pretend you're both married. Or you can both be singles. Have fun with flirtatious talking and delicious touching under the table. At some point in the evening, one of you can suggest going back for coffee. When you get home, keep up the role play and do something new sexually.

DOCTORS AND NURSES

It doesn't matter which of you plays the patient and which of you plays the doctor or nurse, but this role play is fantastic for lots of flirty-dirty talk. You don't need to buy a medical outfit from an adult store—instead, use your imagination. All you need is a sofa or bed for the patient to relax on while you pretend to look for what's wrong with them. This gives you an opportunity to explore their erogenous zones! I'm sure you will think of ways to cure what ails them.

YOUR CAR HAS BROKEN DOWN

Playing the role of helpless female, you pretend your car has broken down and you've knocked on this stranger's door for help—obviously something you wouldn't do in real life! But that's the point of fantasy role play. This role play can take off in a variety of directions. For example, you may have interrupted the homeowner in his shower. He comes to the door wrapped only in a towel. Because of the nature of the role play, you don't actually need a car or costumes.

HORNY FARMER

Pretend to be a hiker who has stopped at a local farm to ask directions. The farmer is a very earthy man who gets suggestive with you almost immediately. He invites you in for coffee and a slice of cake. You can make this as rowdy and earthy as you want. Perhaps the farmer is great at milking cows and makes suggestive remarks about his breast technique! You can run with whatever takes your fancy.

THE BOSS

All you need is a table that can pass for a desk and you're away with this one. You've arrived as the prospective candidate for a job interview. The boss starts flirting with you. He or she (whichever one of you wants to play the boss) asks to see what special skills you have to offer the appointment. You can demonstrate your special skills.

THE RANDY REPAIRMAN

Put him in jeans and a T-shirt and you're halfway to creating this role play. All you have to do is play the damsel in distress and he pretends he can fix anything. Using a simple ploy like sitting down and discussing the work to be done, you can let your skirt ride up and then flirt with each other. It won't be long before his power tool is put to good use!

THE COWBOY

With country music and line-dancing being so popular, lots of men long for the cowboy lifestyle. Instead of a whole lifestyle, they can just get a little sexy by putting on a Western accent and a swagger. Obviously cowboys are lonely and in need of a little home-comfort! So relax and chat each other up in this fantasy scenario that easily becomes a role play.

THE CRIMINAL ON THE RUN

Bring out your bad and crazy side and pretend to be a criminal on the loose who comes across a lonely woman. Pretend that you've broken in and she's shocked and horrified. But you charm her with your cunning ways. So you end up making passionate love because she realizes it's your only chance of one last night of passion before the police find you and put you back in prison.

I hope these examples show how much can be done with a fantasy role play without the need for costumes, etc. Remember that simple props from around the house can be used to add "reality" to role plays—just put that imagination to good use!

Fantasies gone wrong

As I mentioned at the start of this chapter, your fantasy life has the potential to become a problem if it overwhelms your relationship. It's important to keep fantasy and role play in perspective. That is, they're fantastic strands to your sex life and shouldn't become the whole point of sex. They are part of your sexual repertoire, enhancing your sex life, never dominating it.

If you feel your fantasy life, or that of your lover's, is getting out of control, do not hide from this. It will get out of control if you don't talk about it. From Chapter 4 you should now have the skills necessary to talk honestly and openly about sex.

365 Erotic Secrets for Sensational Sex is about generating pleasure for you and your lover, and forming that revolutionary attitude toward your sex life. Part of this revolutionary attitude is to be open to new ideas, for example, your lover's sexual fantasy life, and to know when to set boundaries on things that turn you off.

NINE

Sensationally Advanced Sex-play

When you think of sex, what do you think of? Most people think of sex as something that's essentially short-term pleasure or sexual-tension release. Even when in a long-term relationship they simply think of sex as something that, for example, "We'll be doing tonight," or as an "event" that they and their lover will be having on Saturday morning, etc.

In other cases, some long-term couples use sex to patch over relationship problems as they arise. Although it's fun at the time to have "make-up sex" this can sometimes be damaging to a relationship because a couple uses passion instead of communication to sort things out. Eventually relationship-rot destroys their enjoyment of make-up sex. Another potential issue in the long term is that many people lack the foresight or skills to deepen their sexual knowledge and enhance their sexual repertoire. They end up in a boring sexual routine.

I'd like to revolutionize the way you think about sex over the long-term in a relationship. This might be less important in the short-term, for example as in a vacation romance, because people having a fling obviously hope that sex is going to be fun and tend to let go of any inhibitions. They do this because there's no real worry about what their new and temporary lover is going to think of them. After all, you're both there for sexual pleasure.

Usually in a fling/one-night stand you're simply concerned with enjoying the moment. Which is how it should be as long as you're using safer-sex techniques and you both understand it's just a fling. However, over the longer term you should feel just as free to experiment with more advanced techniques and lose your inhibitions, too. But there are many reasons why people don't do this over the long-term, as I've mentioned. For example, they slip into a sexual routine. But also it's due to things like troubles they face over time that can be related to, for example work or their relationship and the other things that result in Sex Symptoms as I mentioned in the first chapter.

I'm going to outline a number of what I'd call advanced sexual techniques. I say advanced because in comparison to what I call "vanilla" sex techniques they're a little more sophisticated, intimate, daring or elaborate. Now that we've come this far I'm simply going to describe them in list form so you can select which you'd like to try. Think of this as a treasure chest of a chapter or even a chocolate box. You can dip in and out, or pick and choose little treasures to try as you feel like it.

Things to consider first

- Attitude is very important to successfully explore more advanced techniques with your lover. Being positive, open-minded, and suggesting things in a non-threatening way is important for you both.
- From time to time all couples should look to try something new to keep their sexual relationship fresh.
- Taking turns making suggestions will keep the balance in your relationship. Together you can read through this chapter and each highlight the things you want to try. Then alternate whose suggestions you choose to try.
- Make each other feel safe and secure about saying "No" to a new suggestion. You should both agree that if you say "No" to trying something new, you're not saying your lover would be a turn-off doing it but rather the actual technique is a turn-off.
- Finally, this is not a definitive list by any means. The things I suggest might spark off your own ideas—go for it!

Sex-play suggestions that will keep your lust alive

SHAVEN-HAVENS

Time to get a little daring and shave each other's pubic hair. Not only does this generate trust but it certainly deepens intimacy. Never shave each other when you've been drinking or taking recreational drugs—you don't want any unfortunate cuts! Begin by having a warm, sensual shower. Then take turns to lie back and be intimately groomed. First trim excess pubic hair, particularly on him, as men's pubes can grow rather long. Then shave their genitals gently with either some sensitive-care hair conditioner or sensitive-skin shaving gel. You may not be able to get into every little fold of her vagina so you can finish off by tweezing any stray hairs (if she feels comfortable with this). Enjoy the sense of freedom and the extra sensitivity to touch that shaving gives you.

If you hate the itchy re-growth then simply trim your pubic hair closely. Of course, many people feel too inhibited to have their lover trim or shave them, so don't forget that there are many salons for both men and women who will do all sorts of trimming and waxing to your particular requirements. Why not turn this into a surprise and book a salon appointment and have your pubes shaped into something fun and sexy.

GO WILD

Wear old (but clean and neat!) stockings and a dress or top. Suggest that in the height of passion your lover rips them off you just like in an old-fashioned bodice-ripper. This can be fantastic as Sex-play for its own sake or as part of a role play/fantasy scenario. If, for example, she has a fantasy that he's a pirate and he's captured her, the fair maiden, then ripping open her dress will fit right in. Or if, perhaps, he'd like to pretend to be the dominant office manager who rips off her skirt and ravishes her, using clothes like this will add to the effect.

LUSCIOUS LOLLIPOPS

For more fun with ice-play buy the long ice-cube trays (from any kitchenware department or shop) to make ice-pops. These can be traced around the body easier than ice-cubes (despite this, ice-cubes are fun too!). The daring woman might like one slipped up inside her. And the daring man might want one slipped up his backside.

Sensational touching suggestions

LIGHT AS A FEATHER

As mentioned previously, you can get creative with touching. I've already mentioned feathering to you. Let's take it one step further. Drizzle some wonderful lubricant around her clitoris and then slowly circle it with the tip of the feather.

Taking a commercially prepared feather (that's clean!) swirl it gently through the oil. For example, if you've drizzled oil down your lover's breasts you may take the feather and draw it around the base of the breasts—gathering some of the oil on its tip—then drawing the oily tip up the breast to the nipple, flicking the end of it. She'll relish the wonderful sensations of feathering just as a man will. Then trace the feather up and down her outer and inner labia. You can drive her completely crazy with this technique. For him, use a feather around the base of his glans. Pull back his foreskin gently, if he has it, and lightly circle the feather tip, with the lubricant, around the base of his glans and then up to his urethral opening. Continue feathering up and down this area.

EROTIC SKIN-BRUSHING

Get creative and use a kitchen basting brush (again, clean!) or artist's brush and gently swirl sensual oil, moisturising cream, chocolate sauce, or anything that you like over your lover's body. Gently brush your choice of liquid over your lover's skin. Give them some "buttocks-bliss" by brushing gently between them! Turn it into a game and paint some numbers on to their body. Use chocolate sauce or something else edible like body paints. Your lover then has to lick from number to number in chronological order.

♭ SENSATIONAL SEX SECRET

Don't forget to apply erotic touching techniques to all your lover's little erogenous zones like their ears, the back of their neck, or even inside their wrists.

FANTASTIC FEASTS

There are a couple of places in *365 Erotic Secrets for Sensational Sex* where I mention getting sexy with food, including the next chapter. Here I want you to indulge each other's sexy food passions. Let's say she has a fetish for French pastries. You can buy a fresh cream eclair, split it open and wrap it around his penis. With small nibbles she slowly eats it off him. As he feels her lips, teeth (be gentle!) and tongue making their way through the pastry he'll get more and more aroused. Or he can turn her into an ice-cream sundae. Lay her on the bed with a towel underneath her bottom. Part her legs and spoon ice-cream, chocolate sauce and whipped cream over her vagina. Slowly lap it up, teasing her as you go. Pretty much any food can become sexy. For example, she may like a ring-doughnut but she should slip it around his semi-erect penis and eat the sugary doughnut from around him. Or slip your favorite bar of chocolate in between her labia allowing it to start to melt from her body heat. Then carefully lap it out. Share a shower after sexy food play to remove any crumbs, etc.

TIME TO GET HOT

But first a warning: many lovers enjoy testing their pleasure–pain barrier by using hot wax. You can get burned and you need to be very careful. Don't try this when under the influence of alcohol or drugs. Only indulge this desire with a lover you can trust! If you have delicate skin, this is certainly not the technique for you to play around with. You can alternate wax and ice play to create different sensations. Try using birthday candles, which have wax that drips more slowly. Use good quality candles and begin by testing droplets of the wax on the inside of your wrist to ensure it's not too hot.

Begin from a height of about a meter to allow the wax to cool enough before it hits your skin. Either keep ice or a cool, wet cloth handy if you or your lover find the wax too hot. Make sure no drops of burning wax land on the skin or on, for example, the bedsheets with the potential to start a fire. You have been warned!

BALLOON PLAY

This technique will help him develop the skills to be gentler when required. After massaging some lovely oil into each other's stomachs and breasts, blow up an ordinary balloon to about three-quarters full. Put this between you and make love while trying to keep it in place. You'll both have to be careful and if he's on top he'll have to be extra careful not to pop the balloon.

BREAST IS BEST

We girls are guilty of thinking that actually he's not going to get off on a tit-job. Believe me, men love getting dirty with your breasts. Lie back and squirt loads of luscious lube over your breasts and his penis. Using your hands at the sides of your breasts, push them up together. He kneels over you and slips his penis between your breasts. He does the thrusting while you urge him on. Make him feel like a real stud by gasping at the "gorgeousness" of his penis thrusting up toward your face. Don't worry if your breasts are on the small side—as you push them together, you can close your fingertips over the top of the gap forming a complete orifice for him to thrust in between. Your little boobs and fingertips laced together will provide him with plenty of stimulation. Agree in advance if he's allowed to come all over your breasts or if you want him to withdraw and come on your stomach or into a tissue.

PERIOD PLEASURE

When it comes to sex when a woman has her period, people vary tremendously in their attitudes. Some women love it, believing a good orgasm helps with period pains. Other women would be mortified to have sex during their period. Men equally have diverse attitudes. However, if you're going to have fun when you're on a "rag," you can get some fantastic Beppy Action Tampons which look like a large pink marshmallow that you insert into the vagina. They're designed to prevent staining the sheets during sex and allow comfort at the same time. You can get them from the Love Honey website that will be in the contacts list at the end of the book.

INTIMATE INSERTION

I'll be describing all sorts of sex toys in the next chapter, including love eggs, anal plugs and beads. Here I want you to try some truly sensational and intimate Sex-play. For her: She lies on her back while he sits astride her facing her feet. Using loads of lubricant he massages her labia and vagina before inserting some love eggs for her to wear. Or he may slip some anal beads into her anus. It can be a huge turn-on with him having complete control and them not having face-to-face contact. Now for him: He lies on his back while she sits astride him facing his feet. It's his turn to have lots of lubricant rubbed from his perineum to his anus. When he's ready, she slips anal beads or a plug into him.

TICKLE HIS PICKLE

Give him some oral pleasure with a twist. Once you've got him nice and erect and you've been licking him up and down his shaft, slip a fingertip vibrator on to your finger. With lots of lubricant guide it around the base of his glans very gently. This tickling sensation will drive him crazy.

PLEASE YOURSELF BY USING HIM

Since lots of men simply don't understand that women can have a lovely orgasm through simply grinding their clitoris and clitoral region, why not use his body as the perfect implement to grind against? When you're lying together caressing and kissing, use his thigh or pelvis, or turn him over and use his buttocks to grind against. When a woman gets herself off in this earthy and abandoned way, he'll get incredibly excited!

Sensational little finger techniques

As well as the wonderful touching techniques I outlined for you in the chapter on oral sex, here are a few more tempting touching techniques to try. These require some finesse when it comes to giving your lover sensational pleasure.

THE SNAKE

Having manually stimulated his lover's vagina, he should try The Snake. Once she's well lubricated, he can try using two fingers held tightly together. Curving them slightly upward, he gently wiggles them from side to side to apply a gentle, vibrating-type pressure to the inside of her vaginal walls. Since The Snake gives a sensation similar to the motion of a vibrator on slow speed, it's perfect for the woman who is shy of trying a vibrator—or if the man feels threatened by her using a vibrator.

CHANGING OF THE GUARD

Be it left or right, people tend to use their preferred hand when touching their lover's genitals. This means they can miss out on alternative sensations that'll give their lover pleasure. By simply changing hands, it'll create a different sensation. While you are touching his penis, testicles and perineum, or her clitoral region, labia, vagina and perineum, change midway to your other hand. Obviously don't do this if they're about to reach orgasm.

SUBTLE TOUCH

Why not try a touching technique that's slightly fetishistic? Slip on a pair of gloves of any texture you prefer—soft and velvety, smooth and silky, firm and leathery. With lots of lubricant—and ensuring the gloves are clean (!) so your lover isn't irritated by them—start teasing them slowly. They'll love the different sensations created on their erogenous zones.

WHOLE PALM PLEASURE

Use the whole of the palm of your hand covered in a luscious lubricant to add an earthy dimension to manual Sex-play. He can spread her legs and use the whole palm of his hand to gently massage across her pubis, clitoral region and introitus, and continue down her perineum. He can use his free hand to hold open her thighs. Many women love the sense of being under the control of his touch. She can do the same to him. She can sit astride him facing his feet, open his legs and use generous sweeping motions with her whole palm around his testicles and perineum, down under his buttocks, and back up over the whole of his shaft. While she's doing this he can massage her buttocks for extra pleasure.

⚶ SENSATIONAL SEX SECRET

Always warm up your hand before any manual Sex-play. Rub some lubricant or massage oil between your hands so your lover's skin doesn't get a chilly shock!

LIQUID SENSATIONS

People like to be well lubricated, all over their genitals, but also wherever they feel like it on their body because it makes sex lovely and slushy. You can have fun with wet-play of different types. For example, spread out a towel on your bed and ask your lover to lie back and open their legs. With a warm bowl of water and clean face cloth, squeeze droplets over her labia or his penis and testicles. Or while they're lying back, squirt some lubricant along the top of their pubic bone and allow it to drip down over their genitals before you gently massage it in. This can be incredibly sensual when done with confidence and care.

While sharing a bath, have your lover sit back and open their legs and allow water from the showerhead to gush over their pubic bone. The warm water cascading down over her labia or his penis and testicles will feel wonderful. Ensure you don't point the showerhead upward into her vagina, as there's a very small chance that you could force an air bubble up inside her.

SEDUCTIVE AND SILKY

Some women are so sensitive they can't stand direct touch. This gives a man the perfect excuse to fondle her sensuously through silky fabric. Turn this small act into a sensational seduction. Many women masturbate against a silky pillow or with their silky panties on. Based on this principle the two of you can heighten her enjoyment of being touched very carefully by, for example, running a silken scarf across her clitoral region and labia. While you do Sex-play like this why not whisper in her ear how she's as soft as the silky fabric.

Then ask her to roll on her side and spread her legs while you pull a silken scarf back and forth across her labia and clitoris. You can run the scarf back and forth over her pubic bone, down her labia, and up over her buttocks. Add in some erotic flicks with your tongue against her skin.

You might find the man in your life likes this sort of sensation against his testicles and perineum. With the same method, gently slide your silky panties or bathrobe sash across his skin. Then slide the fabric across the nipples, down to the genitals and over the buttocks. For a little little of "gender bending," let him slip into your panties and stroke him through the silky fabric.

Continue this theme of using silky materials for some tempting strip fun. Turn down the lights and put on a little mood music.

Stand in front of your lover and go for the sexy stripper look by swaying your hips as you pull that silky cloth between your thighs. Next run it over your breasts teasing your nipples so that they become erect.

Sensational looking

Stripping—Now we're getting to a little of performance! You can put on a sensational performance for your lover. It takes practice and confidence as well as some courage, but believe me, men love watching their lover strip.

But with the rise of the Chippendales over a decade ago and the popularity of the film *The Full Monty*, women love it when men strip for them, too.

Here are some tips to get you started:
1.   While on your own, practice some moves you feel comfortable with.
2.   Use the kind of music that you feel good moving to. Whether it's the classic mood music, thumping rock beat or a smooth R&B number, you have to like it.
3.   Practice in clothes that are easy to strip off. You'll have more confidence wearing clothing you feel sexy in but that's also easy to remove.
4.   Once you know what you feel sexy in and which moves you feel comfortable with, leave the CD in the player ready to go.

5.   To create the best possible atmosphere, have some candles in place for soft lighting.

6.   When you practice, use your imagination and pretend you're a lap dancer or male stripper. Visualize the sorts of moves they do and add them to your repertoire.

7.   Don't forget to practice touching and fondling yourself, and thinking about the things you'd say if your lover was watching you.

8.   You'll feel most confidence with slow and sensual moves. Don't try anything too complicated!

9.   When it comes to the moment, dim the lights, light the candles, start the CD and ask your lover to sit in a chair.

10. Have fun with it—you could tie their hands to the chair so there's no touching. Push his head between your breasts or he can swing his penis in front of your eyes.

11. Lay down some playful rules, like you can fondle and touch them but they can't touch you!

12. If you both feel daring, you can do some "research" for your strip routines by going to watch some stripping together. Couples often find it a huge turn-on to watch strippers in action.

13. If you still lack confidence, women can find strip classes in most cities to build body-confidence.

A ROOM WITH A VIEW

For an evening of erotic stimulation there are now a number of lap-dancing and strip clubs that welcome couples. Many women are turned-on by watching erotic dancing. As a couple, you may get incredibly excited, charge home and have the best sex you've had in ages. However, if you're a man who wants to suggest a night out like this to your partner, please do so tactfully.

NYATAIMORI NIGHTS

There are a few Japanese restaurants around that offer this slice of Eastern eroticism. Customers are allowed to eat Japanese delicacies off girls' naked bodies. Be warned as no touching is allowed! Again this is the sort of night out you need to suggest in a loving way and not in a manner that makes her think you can't wait to see a woman's naked body in front of you.

GET PLAYFUL WITH PORN

Many people take the odd Polaroid snap of each other in states of undress. But it's becoming a real art-house phenomenon to make your own porn movies. Before you start, agree that the films are to be kept under lock and key. If you're in a rocky relationship I'd recommend thinking twice, as you don't want to have a break-up and find out that your "home video" ends up on the Internet, posted there by your angry ex.

But if you are going to film each other, it's worth spending a little time thinking about subtle lighting and which angles your bodies look sexiest from. Do some test shots when you're not in the heat of passion, but simply pose for the camera to get an idea of angles. When it comes to watching professional porn, I've got a number of places to recommend to shop for this in the website and contacts list at the end of the book.

Sensational interaction

PC PLEASURE

Having cybersex has become a very popular pastime. Unfortunately, it's a pastime that has also destroyed many relationships. This happens when one person thinks that having a little cyber fun is not harmful and their partner sees it as a form of infidelity. If you're single, go ahead and try it. If you're in a couple, why not liven up the times you're apart by trying it. If you're part of a couple but want to go it alone with your computer and a webcam, I think it's only fair to let your other half know that you're experimenting with cybersex.

All you need to get started is to sit at your computer with or without webcams and microphones. And having found a suitable person to interact with through cyberspace, you tell them what you'd like or perhaps what you fantasize about. Typing messages back or speaking into a microphone allows you to give as much detail as you want.

Many people say they feel less inhibited having cybersex. Others claim that they are less likely to be looking for an affair if they have this extra release that gives them a little bit of a buzz. I say to them that they're simply looking for an excuse to make their partner feel they have to allow them a little cybersex—because of course most partners don't want their lover to stray. Outwardly they rationalize that cybersex isn't really cheating, but inside many feel it is. Some people enjoy it because it's easy and accessible at any time of the day or night that they are free.

It's important that once you've logged on, you do not give away any personal information because you never know who's at the other end of your cybersex communication. Just as with Internet or agency dating, people do lie about themselves. Never arrange to meet anyone that you've been having cybersex with unless you use the standard dating precautions of taking a friend along with you and meeting in a public place during the daytime. Certainly the biggest drawback from an emotional and psychological perspective is that cybersex uses up the time that you could be spending looking for an actual (rather than a virtual) partner. Particularly if you have an addictive nature and find yourself logging in repeatedly, your life can become a very sad and solitary one. I don't want to put a complete downer on cybersex, but I think it's best used sparingly if you're single, and together if you're a couple that happen to be apart but are both at your computers and want to have the equivalent of phone sex.

PHONE SEX

Having just mentioned it, you can have a lot of truly raunchy fun
with phone sex. Again there is this element of letting go of your
inhibitions because you're not face-to-face. People tell me they
feel much freer talking on the phone. They feel more willing to
share intimate fantasies and talk dirty. Early in a relationship it
may be particularly helpful for you to learn communication skills
with your new lover by getting hot together on the phone. Just
make sure you then learn to take this sexy chat into face-to-face
action with them.

REALLY DIRTY DANCING

With the craze for Latin-American and ballroom dancing, why
not take up some dancing at home? The sexiest dances include
the ceroc, lambada, mambo, paso doble, and merengue. As you'll
be doing your dirty dancing at home, why not strip down to your
sexiest lingerie for her and pants for him? Turn down the lights,
turn up the rhythms and swivel your bodies together until you're
lightly perspiring. Turn it into a fantasy session where one of you
pretends to be the sexy Latin dance instructor.

G-spot stimulation

I've touched on the "come over here" technique in the chapter on
oral sex, but let's take another look at the G Spot generally.
Potentially you can stimulate her G Spot during oral, manual or
penetrative techniques. What you need most is to explore her

potential to enjoy G-Spot stimulation. A word of warning: Some women claim not to have any sensitivity in the G-Spot area and that is absolutely fine. She should be under no pressure to find a G Spot. About seventy percent of women claim to have sensitivity in this area—the front inner wall of their vagina. Usually they feel it during penetrative sex with rear-entry positions like Spoons or Doggy style. This is when the penis is thrusting against the front vaginal wall. Again, if a woman does not feel or recognize such sensitivity, it doesn't mean she's any less sexy, or is going to enjoy sex less than the woman who has G-Spot sensitivity.

To begin exploring whether she has G-Spot sensitivity she needs to feel free to experiment in any way she wants. When she's aroused and lubricated you can begin with the "come over here" finger position. Or use a vibrator specifically shaped for G-Spot stimulation and enjoy a gentle feel around. If you two are feeling hot why not use slow, circular, massaging motions with your penis? As you manipulate your penis, ask her about the different sensations she's experiencing.

GO FOR THE GROOVE

Men often think of thrusting during penetration as a simple in-out, back and forth movement. It's not only that, as you can get incredibly creative with your thrusting. One way to get a woman completely aroused is by teasing her through very slow, circular thrusting. This can be thrusting from positions where you face each other or from behind, in which case circular thrusting is ideal for your G-spot "investigations."

Definitely introduce a little sex chat into this experience when you try thrusting in different ways. An easy idea is to pretend you're a massage expert and you need to massage her with your penis in the special way that only you know how. Why not start in Doggy position with you behind her, holding her hips. Start moving your pelvis in slow circular motions—around and around deep inside her vagina. Ask her how your special "massage" is feeling. Get her to tell you what movements feel the most sensational.

THE U SPOT

Five years ago, research discovered a little place called the "U" spot—which some women found more exciting than their G spot. The U spot is a little surface area of delicate skin located above the opening of the urethral canal about a half-centimeter below the clitoris. The urethral opening itself is just above the opening to the vagina, the introitus.

Many women find that light touching or "rubbing" of this little spot (with the finger, tongue or nose even!) is like rubbing the genie's magic lamp. Sex research suggests that pressure on the U spot might lead to a build up of secretions in the periurethral glands inside the vagina. This in turn might be associated with the elusive female ejaculation.

You need to be very careful stimulating this intimate spot as over-stimulation may lead to irritation of the urethral canal. This can easily lead to cystitis. Why not use some fantasy play to explore this area. Pretend you're a doctor that needs to proceed carefully with a detailed examination of her U-spot area. If stimulation of this area doesn't do it for her, then don't worry about it.

AROUSE HER A-ZONE

Sex research now considers the entire area of the anterior fornix, or A-zone, as underrated. This is the area of her front (stomach side) vaginal wall from the G Spot upward to her cervix. The whole area has nerves and tissues that can be stimulated with different sex positions and sex toys. You may find that with some of the circular thrusting techniques, she enjoys getting this whole, upper front wall stimulated. Certainly it's under-stimulated with the traditional man-on-top missionary style position. But you wouldn't just stick to that position now would you?

FEMALE EJACULATION

As I've just mentioned, this is an elusive and unusual occurrence that is hotly debated by sex researchers. That said, as I've asked you to take a revolutionary new attitude to your sexual enjoyment, please do experiment with this. The best way to do so is ensure your G Spot and A-zone are well stimulated and aroused. You might find it's easier to stimulate these areas with a sex toy with a flatter end that can stimulate this whole area. Once highly aroused, if you feel the pressure to pee, try to hold back, as it may well be the build up of fluid associated with female ejaculation that is not urine. As well as this essential stimulation, you need to let

your mind completely relax as you come to orgasm. If fluid is ejac-
ulated when you orgasm, a simple smell test will tell you whether
it was pee or whether you've had a female ejaculatory experience.
I stress yet again, that no one should feel any pressure to aim for
this. This is not the gold star of sexual achievement. This is simply
something you could experiment with if you're inclined.
Otherwise, quite frankly, who cares and don't let any of your least-
inhibited, and most-experimental friends tell you otherwise!

Tempting teasing

If I can help you develop one new attitude in your sex life then I
hope it would be an attitude of stimulating temptation with a
teasing quality toward your lover. Temptation and teasing form
the basis of eroticism and are hugely underrated. Many lovers get
to the point of penetrative sex and simply forget that a little teasing goes a long way! Teasing helps draw out penetrative sex, an
excellent thing if either lover needs more time. Partial penetration is an excellent way of doing this. There are a number of ways
either lover can control this.

TECHNIQUES FOR HER TO TRY:

- Sit astride him and rub your well-lubricated labia up and
  down the length of his shaft until he's ready to burst.
  Take your time and use gentle pelvic thrusts for another
  sensation.

- Or if you're in The Spoons or other rear-entry position, carefully take hold of the shaft of his penis and again rub the tip of his penis up and down your clitoral region, and in and out of your introitus without allowing full penetration.

- For even more delicious pleasure after the first few strokes of penetration, either the man or the woman can take control again and move back to these partial, teasing techniques. These delaying tactics can be explosive and with a little imagination you'll discover small variations that yield new sensations.

HE CAN TRY THE FOLLOWING TECHNIQUES:

- While he's on top of her he can tease her clitoris with the end of his penis. Either straddling her, sitting astride her, or kneeling between her legs he can hold the shaft of his penis and simply rub it up and down or in slow, sensuous, circular motions. Beginning with her clitoral region, he can then move his strokes down her labia and partially enter her introitus.

- In the shower or standing nude or partially clothed, again he may nudge the tip of his penis between her legs and over her clitoral region and use a variety of gentle rubbing motions to stimulate and partially enter her.

Bound and gagged

Thinking about teasing your lover and partial penetration brings me quite nicely to Bondage-play. That's because the main element of Bondage-play is about teasing. Yes, teasing that involves ties, sashes, ropes, handcuffs and blindfolds, etc., but teasing all the same. Aside from the teasing quality, there are a lot of erotic features with Bondage-play and part of that is fantasy and role play. Many people have bondage fantasies and those who tend to get involved in real bondage often use role play as the catalyst to a bondage session.

People who indulge in Bondage-play say it allows them a lot of emotional freedom because they can experiment with different roles. They can take the dominant role, submissive role and cross between the two. A lot of people get confused between bondage and dominant/submissive Sex-play, which is different from sadomasochistic (S&M) practices. Let me clarify this for you. Bondage-play involves restraint, control, developing sexual tension, teasing and sometimes giving verbal commands to a lover in order to get them to "submit" to your demands. S&M is more likely to involve real pain and degradation. Having said that, different individuals will have their own boundaries and definitions, or some lovers will simply lump such practices all together. I'm not going to get into heavy S&M practices here so you'll need a specialist book if you're interested in those. I hope though that you'll feel free to experiment with some of the suggestions I make here.

Before you get started, I have to warn you that lots of people will get in a panic simply at the mention of Bondage-play. They wrongly assume it's going to be heavy sadism and masochism—which it is not. With people's anxieties in mind, make sure when you start suggesting things to a lover that they understand what you mean. This requires the most basic communication skills where you clearly outline the sorts of things you have in mind. To make your conversation a little sexier you can put it in the context of a fantasy you've had.

A FEW GROUND RULES

Here are some little rules to keep your Bondage-play sexy and safe:

- ❦ You must have a code word! This is a neutral word agreed upon by the two of you that tells the other that no matter what you're doing you want to stop. It must be a neutral word because we say so many things during the height of passion that you don't want this word to get confused with something you're raving about. It can't be "No" because sometimes we say "No" as part of a role play. When your lover hears the code word they have to stop. If you don't trust them to stop, you shouldn't be practicing any Bondage-play with them.

- ❦ Never give in to pressure to do something you find frightening or that would turn you off. As I've already said, no one should try anything sexual that turns them off, but this is particularly true when it comes to these sorts of practices. Many people think if they talk through an idea with their lover then that's not pressure. However, there are subtle forms of pressure. The subtlest type of pressure is where one lover wants to please a lover by giving into a suggestion—even if in their own mind it turns them off or causes them anxiety.

- Don't do dangerous practices! Many people are fascinated by the idea of auto-asphyxiation, where they restrict their own airways or try to restrict their airways with a lover. My message is quite simple: don't restrict airways.

- Don't try Bondage-play when you've been drinking or taking recreational drugs. This may sound very over-the-top, but alcohol and drugs alter your inhibitions and ideas of what's safe and not safe. Drugs and alcohol can also change your pain threshold.

- Do not leave people unattended. If you've restrained your lover, you must untie them if you're leaving the room. It might sound like a joke to try to scare them by leaving them tied up, but accidents can happen.

- Know your knots. Practice makes perfect and it also makes perfect sense if you're thinking about tying up a lover. You need to know how to undo any thing you've tied. I'd always recommend tying simple bows. Believe me, it's not funny when you're both ready for hot sex and you can't get the restraints undone on your lover's wrists!

- If something feels uncomfortable, it will probably get worse later on. Make sure you or your lover is comfortable when, for example, your hands are tied behind the back. If it feels a little uncomfortable now, there's a good chance it will be painful later.
- Have fun tying each other up, but don't restrain any area for too long. Particularly when using something like a cock ring, which should never be used by a man for more than twenty minutes. Tie bows and not knots!
- Keep it clean! Don't forget to consider hygiene when someone is, for example, tied up and you're both aroused. That's when it's easy to forget common rules of hygiene. When you've used sex toys in your Bondage-play, for example, your restrained lover has asked to be pleasured with a vibrator, it's easy to get carried away. You may forget when you're both enjoying yourselves that you can't use the same sex toy to vaginally stimulate them if you've been using it in her anus. Any sex toy, etc., used in the anal area should then be washed before further use. You can solve this problem by keeping two sex toys at hand, with one just for anal pleasure and the other for other erogenous zones.

Being restrained in Bondage-play heightens sexual tension. As the restrained person can do little more than wriggle around, trying to get the dominant lover to stimulate them, their sexual tension increases. It becomes a game where they want some relief from this tension but the dominant person doesn't allow it. If you want to try a little bondage play without taking it too seriously, here are some suggestions to try partial restraint:

- Adult shops and Internet sites (I'll provide you with the details of many places to shop at the end of the book) supply a wide range of restraints. If you're a newcomer to Bondage-play, why not experiment with a few items from around the home? Bear in mind that unless something's been made to be a sex toy, you should be careful not to use something that can harm you or your lover. Try using silky stockings or tights, a bathrobe sash or scarf, ribbon that you'd usually use for wrapping presents, even belts—particularly if they're made of soft leather.

- Have some fun with the comfortable and ready-made "bondage sheets." With Velcro straps for the ankles and wrists, these have both a positive and negative side. On the positive side you can play safely with no knots to get tangled up with. At the same time, the downside is the "manufactured" feel which puts some people off who'd rather experience the spontaneity of grabbing whatever is handy to bind or be bound with.

EXPERIMENT WITH THESE RESTRAINTS

- Let's begin with the hands either tied together or separately. There are all sorts of handcuffs and restraints available as well as the soft and silky sashes to use that I mentioned above. Alternatively, you can tie your lover's hands separately to the headboard or even with long enough sashes to the legs of a bed or chair.

- Next, you can bind their wrists together in front or behind them. It's important to consider your lover's comfort if their hands are tied behind!

- Moving a little further up the arms, try tying their elbows together. You can pin the elbows back with a sash/belt, which can be very erotic as it forces the woman's breasts out if she's the one being dominated. However, you won't have much play-time before this gets uncomfortable.

- Moving on to the legs, you can bind your lover's knees. You can get an unnaturally tight squeeze for penetrative sex by doing this to her knees. This is definitely worth trying if you're into experimenting with different sensations.

- Ankles have been considered erotic since Victorian times so let's not neglect those. Be careful, as they can be very ticklish! Try strapping your lover's ankles together, which will give them the sense they can't escape from the dastardly and dominant Sex-play you're about to do to them. You can tie their feet together or separately to a headboard or legs of a chair.

- Get seriously dominant by forcing your lover to drop their inhibitions. You can do this by exposing their genitals during Bondage-play that literally puts their most intimate parts on display. For example, ease your lover back over the back of a comfy armchair. Now tie their legs apart with their ankles bound to the chair legs. This completely exposes them for teasing orally or with sex toys, etc. Not for the faint-hearted! Remember, tie bows, not knots!

SENSORY DEPRIVATION

It's amazing how you can heighten the sensitivity of your lover's skin by blindfolding them. Once you remove one sense (sight in this case) the other senses start to work harder to compensate. Blindfolds can be used in many ways. For a couple who have lost touch with sensuality, it's a good way of gently exploring their bodies and reconnecting intimately. Or blindfolds can be used to heighten erotic techniques like "feathering" and "ice play" already mentioned. When it comes to bondage and domination, blindfolds will give you an extra edge to your Sex-play.

Instead of a blindfold, you could wear a mask for Bondage-play. Though it's definitely not a good idea to scare your lover by jumping out of the closet with a gimp mask on! What I'm talking about are exotic masks like the ones you might see at the Venice Carnival or the more fetishist types of masks. Anything that the dominant person decides to use to obscure their face is fine as long as it's not frightening. By obscuring your eyes or complete face, you lend a sense of mystery to your Sex-play. It also makes it easier to enjoy a fantasy that you're being dominated by a stranger. If the dominant party wears a mask, the submissive person who's been bound might also want to be gagged. I cannot stress how much you need to be careful and exercise caution so that a gag doesn't slip and cause choking.

DRESS FOR BONDAGE BLISS

You might make a sexier impression if you choose one sensational piece of bondage gear rather then kitting yourself out head-to-toe in it. You can begin by wearing the colors associated with domination such as black and scarlet. Add to this your highest heels and you'll add to the atmosphere.

If you and your partner get into Bondage-play it could be worthwhile for both of you to invest in some bondage clothing. Everyone has their own preferences and you may prefer clothing in leather, PVC or rubber. You might wear high-heeled, thigh-high boots or stilettos. You might choose black stockings paired with something like a corset, miniskirt or basque. For a man, he may want to get a genital bondage strap (there are loads of varieties!), a slinky thong or one with leather and studs. Any of these things can liven up your Bondage-play. If you're on a budget, make your own bondage-looking gear by cutting holes in your lingerie underwear for your nipples, vagina or penis to show through.

Sadomasochistic practices

As I said earlier, people blur the lines between bondage and domination (B&D) and sadomasochism (S&M). Definition is not so important, but rather how you two feel as lovers about the sort of things you're willing to try. Many people relish a little bit of pain, feeling that it enhances their sexual pleasure. That's why people joke, saying things like, "It hurts so good!"

It's actually the case that some types of pain increase muscle tone. This in turn leaves the skin ready for further stimulation. When you consider historical practices such as self-flagellation during some religious festivities, it would bring people to a state of religious ecstasy. You can understand how this was transferred into sexual ecstasy. In the Middle Ages, when flogging and birching were regularly used as a religious penance, many people actually came to find the heightened state that was released in them pleasurable. This would give rise to a desire for more.

For the purposes of *365 Erotic Secrets for Sensational Sex* I'm only touching on lightweight or "vanilla" S&M. Here are just a few things for you to consider before you get started. Let's begin with the verbal element that goes along with S&M and "discipline." Many find that just hearing their lover bark some orders at them is a turn-on. For example, you may be doing a little of a role play like in the film *The Secretary*. The "boss" is unhappy with the "secretary's" work. He barks an order to her to come over to his desk and bend over. He then threatens punishment. Whether or not he actually spanks her bottom is one thing, but it's the sadistic manner in which he speaks to her that might turn her on. If you both know what the other finds a turn-on and what they find utterly humiliating, this will allow you to get the verbal tone just right.

LET'S GET PHYSICAL

Spanking and whipping are the most popular physical activities in S&M. Most people don't realize it, but because spanking and whipping increases the blood flow to the skin, it actually makes a person more orgasmic. When you increase the blood flow to an area you also heighten sensation there. Drop in a little dirty talk and many people find it incredibly exciting.

Spanking can be done with your hand or anything you can get your hands on! Raid your kitchen for a big wooden spoon, your bathroom for a hair brush, or buy a "spanking paddle" from an adult shop. Some have an optional fur-lined side for a gentler action. It's the same for whipping, which can range from the "very vanilla," for example, with a bathrobe sash, to the "hard-core" with a thin leather whip guaranteed to sting and which most probably will draw blood.

Even if you're not into S&M you might find that a quick smack or slap delivered during sex to the buttocks or thighs may be something your lover enjoys even if they don't want to get into S&M. And as long as you know your lover won't mind. Or you could try a little pinching when your lover reaches orgasm. This can heighten that pain–pleasure threshold in an innocent way. It might also get you two thinking about other erotic pleasures to try. You can experiment with these "vanilla" techniques to sound out how both of you feel and what you might enjoy.

As always, I have a word of warning for you: Always exercise care and common sense when indulging in S&M. For example, you should never whip anything near the eyes for obvious reasons. When it comes to spanking and whipping you need to change locations on your lover's skin to avoid bruising or even permanent damage from repeated spankings/whippings in the form of broken veins and mottled skin. Simply vary where you wield that spanking paddle! Any professional "top" worth their salt knows this (a "top"—or "dom" in some circles—means the person who either dominates or acts sadistically to a "bottom"). A "bottom" (or "sub" for submissive) is the one who seeks pain, humiliation or both.

Be spontaneous and have fun. For example, if you're playing ping-pong, grab the paddle, wink at your lover, and suggest you paddle their little bottom during Sex-play. Or if you're eating something sweet like licorice whips, why not whip your lover's bottom with those instead of using real leather whips?

Fetish lust

The word fetish has entered everyday language and is used loosely to describe something you find a turn on. For example, a man might say, "I get turned on by a woman in PVC" but in fact, he can also be turned on by a woman who isn't wearing it. In the true spirit of a fetish, it would mean he couldn't get turned on unless a woman was wearing PVC. Or if he was good at fantasizing about PVC, then he'd need to imagine her decked out in it from head to toe while having sex. In psychological terms, a true fetish requires the fetish object (or thoughts of it) to be present for the person to achieve sexual arousal.

Fetishes can range from the completely harmless—like men who love women with big breasts and seek out sexual partners endowed with these—to what most people would find bizarre or downright disgusting. When someone has a fetish for something like Scat-play or coprophilia, the rest of us wonder quite rightly how on earth someone could develop such an interest. With careful exploration you can usually uncover the reasons why an extreme or revolting fetish develops. At an anecdotal level, I've discussed with many people why their fetishes have arisen and it can be an interesting process.

Let me simplify what can be a complex process. A fetish may begin when some sort of sexual arousal occurs in the presence of an *unrelated* stimulus. That unrelated stimulus goes on to become sexually charged. A good example of this is the potential origin of a foot fetish. Let's say in childhood, after bath time a boy was placed stomach-down on his mom's knee. While being rubbed dry with a towel he *innocently* received stimulation to his genitals as his genitals were pushed into his mom's lap as she toweled him off. He then started to link sexual arousal with the sight of feet—

because while staring at his mom's feet he was aroused. The two can become forever linked.

Other times, the development of a fetish can become a more complex process when sexual arousal is related to excitement or risk. So, for example, a child might have made a mess in the toilet with his bowel movement and then gets reprimanded. He may feel a thrill of excitement at having been a little naughty. Such early memories can shape what excites us or feels risky (and then something we want to try!) as adults. You can't deny that in a lot of fetish and other Sex-play there's an element of risk. And as our sense of sexuality is formed early in our lives it's easy to see how unusual desires can come from experiences early on. Fetishes can originate later in life, again from the pairing of something that becomes sexually charged but also through the pressure from a lover to try new things that the person then gets excited by.

FUNKY STUFF

Putting aside extreme fetishes, you can have a little of funky fetish fun. There are a few fetish items like a whip or spanking paddle that have become very commonplace. But there are lots of little accessories that go with B&D and S&M. For example, there are all sorts of nipple/genital clamps available to add a little pain/pleasure to your Sex-play. The variety of clamps and chains is quite surprising and they can be used in all sorts of ways. I will suggest a number of things like "cock rings" and anal plugs in

Chapter 10 on sex toys and other little goodies. But many of these things will liven up bondage and/or S&M.

GET SPIKY

Give him the perfect cross between some erotic pain and a back massage. Blindfold him and ask him to lie comfortably on the floor on his stomach. Pad out your carpet with some lush towels or soft blankets for him to lie on. Now test his pain–pleasure zone on his back by gently digging your stiletto heel into it. Next, gently and carefully walk on him with your stilettos. Obviously, he has to let you know when it crosses into being too painful.

THE FETISH FURNITURE

As with most fetish-type interests and practices they tend to be well serviced by manufacturers. This is certainly true for fetish, S&M and B&D furniture from specialist shops. You could furnish an entire dungeon in your back bedroom with furniture made in the form of medieval racks, stocks, punishment chairs, etc. You can even find all sorts of wall and ceiling fixtures for "stringing up" your lover that when used properly won't do permanent damage to them. Such items are particularly good for those of you who want to have a good voyeuristic look at your lover's genitals.

WHEELIE PLEASURE

For some unusual Bondage-play, you can rent a wheelchair for the day. Play Master and Captive and strap them in. There are lots of little bits and bobs to tie things to. A variety of medical suppliers and healthcare organizations rent them out—just don't let them know what you're planning.

WATER SPORTS

Water sports are certainly not to everyone's taste. People who get into water sports tend to like the earthiness or the daring aspect of it and even the humiliation of practices like being urinated on. If you're into this practice, then you can always experiment with it in the shower or bath. This causes less mess and seems less threatening. However, being utterly turned off by the thought of this practice myself, there are a couple of great alternatives. Why not pour warm tea slowly over your lover's back or stomach particularly when they're blindfolded? This will give them the sensation of being urinated on without the "yuck-factor."

I'm not judging those of you that are into water sports but it's certainly not something you should pressure a lover into trying. It is one of those practices that most people are very turned off by. If you are into it, you need to be careful when doing hard-core water-sports-play involving things such as urinating into a tube that's inserted into your lover's vagina or rectum (male or female). You can very easily spread STIs and other nasty germs!

Potentially you risk this even if you give someone a golden shower while you're having a regular shower together. So be careful and play safely.

Anal sex

Practically every man and many woman I've ever spoken to about their secret sexual desires have wondered what the "forbidden fruit" of sexual practices would be like. Traditionally anal sex has been viewed as forbidden despite the fact it's been practiced by various cultures throughout the ages. For example, the ancient Sumerians who had highly enlightened views about sexual practices enjoyed practicing both hetero- and homosexual anal sex. Certainly, without the risk of pregnancy, anal sex gave pleasure long before other forms of birth control were practiced.

Still illegal in some states, anal sex is considered by many to be very taboo or risqué. Many people are not comfortable with the thought of anal sex and, as always, you should respect your lover's wishes if they are simply not interested in trying it. If this is the case, you could ask if they're willing to get into a little Anal-play instead.

This is definitely where my revolutionary approach to opening your mind to new and potentially sensational pleasures comes into play. It's a myth that anal sex must involve full penetration. Many people who try it find that simply a little little of Anal-play is enjoyable. This is a very individual thing, though. For example,

simply giving each other erotic and sensual massage of the buttocks, perineum and inner thigh is a good starting point. You may
then get them to agree to simply a little fingering around
their/your anal opening—as long as you're practicing safer sex
and don't allow contact between your fingers and anus by using
sturdy plastic wrap or a dental dam. You might just find that they
enjoy the manual stimulation around their anus. They might
allow you to slip a finger inside or you both might enjoy a little
kissing and licking around this area. But again they might want to
draw the line at actual penetration by your tongue. Again they
might like you to stimulate around their anus in this way but
again you must use a barrier of some type.

If anal sex is on the agenda for you two, here are some basic
considerations to make it as pleasurable as possible. I'm writing
these tips as if she is going to be the "receiver." However, they
equally apply to a man who wants to be stimulated by a vibrator
or her finger, or if having gay sex:

- Obviously, you will have discussed whether or not she
  wants to try a little anal penetration.
- She'll need to empty her rectum either naturally or with
  the help of a suppository purchased from the drugstore if
  you're going for a full penetration.
- Her anal area and your hands need to be clean before you
  get started. It doesn't matter if you're simply going to
  stimulate her with your finger, any fumbling around means
  you may be touching this delicate, potentially germ-laden,

area. You don't want to introduce infection either from your hands to her, or from her anal area to you.

- Ensure your nails are tidy and clean so they don't cause unnecessary discomfort.

- Being relaxed can make all the difference in anal penetration. Obviously this is particularly true for the person who's going to be penetrated. If she's tense about trying it, or tense about anything else in her life for that matter, there's no way her sphincter will relax. As anal penetration is the exact opposite of what the sphincter and rectum is made for, this is absolutely critical. This means that foreplay should have aroused her thoroughly, meaning she's more likely to be relaxed.

- With the best will in the world, anal penetration can be difficult, so agree that you're going to begin by indulging in a little anal "play" for starters. Why not put a condom or latex glove on your finger, covered in loads of lubricant, and try fingering her anus first? Next insert one finger gently and leave it there without moving it. By leaving it there "resting" it allows the outer anal sphincter to relax. Or you could indulge in a little anilingus, or "rimming" as I've already mentioned. Place a dental dam between your tongue and her anus. Or if you're keen to get some penis action going, then slip a condom on your penis and gently rub the tip of your penis around her anal area and perineum. This might both relax and arouse her.

This takes a lot of trust, so if you can do this, you're probably already on a good vibe to having full anal sex.

- As the anal passage doesn't lubricate itself in the way the vagina does, please apply lots of water-based or condom-friendly lubricant. As well as using lots of lube, ensure the condom is of the pre-lubricated type.

- During Anal-play, re-apply the lubricant as necessary.

- Before attempting penetration, she should expel any wind that may be in her rectum. This prevents embarrassing noises during penetration. A great tip for this is for her to pop into the bathroom, get down on all fours and raise her bottom in the air, which makes it easier to get rid of wind.

- People vary in the sort of position they like, but a good one to try is The Spoons position. Otherwise, as long as she's well supported by lots of pillows/cushions you can try Doggy style. If you're physically fit, you may want to try one of the other more technically difficult positions already outlined in the Positions chapter that give good anal-access. Make sure cushions or other forms of supports don't slip, so she stays comfortable and keeps relaxed.

- Here's another useful tip that some people find it hard to get their head around. As he starts penetration she should try gently expelling wind, as this temporarily relaxes the sphincter making penetration easier.

◆ Even the most willing partner who's happy to try receiving anal sex may experience pain or discomfort for a couple of days afterward.

Many straight men are keen to try anal by being the one to penetrate her. However, he may also want to try being penetrated but might be shy to suggest this. Many straight men worry that their partner will think they're gay if they ask for anal penetration. In actuality, about 30 percent of strap-on dildos are sold to straight couples as opposed to lesbian couples, so you can safely assume that he's the one who's going to be penetrated. So whether or not it's the man or the woman who raises the issue of trying anal sex, he should be reassured that if he's keen to try it, you won't think he's secretly gay. His prostate gland may be stimulated by Anal-play through pressure that can enhance his orgasm. Again, all the above points apply to him too.

People who enjoy anal sex do so because it's a very different sensation to that of vaginal sex. The anus has many nerve endings that obviously are not usually stimulated by something going inward. People also say the experience is enhanced because of the fact that anal sex is still seen as forbidden.

DOUBLE TROUBLE

Some people love the feeling of being completely "filled up." And some lovers might see the following suggestions as the ultimate sexual experience between two people.

For her: Choose her favorite vibrator to insert into her vagina. Once she's enjoying this he penetrates her anally. She can take over controlling the vibrator action while he concentrates on his thrusting.

For him: We can't leave him out of the male-type version of "double trouble," so try this while in The Spoons position with him penetrating her vaginally but from behind. She moves her upper body forwards, bending from the waist so he doesn't lose penetration, but meaning she can reach between their legs and penetrate him with an anal vibrator.

PRO-JOBS

Here's another hot technique that you can thank the sex business for. I've coined the term the pro-job. I've named it this after speaking to professionals in the sex industry for research purposes and have found that many men ask sex workers for this. While giving him a blow-job, you penetrate him anally with your finger. Obviously slip your finger into a latex glove or a condom to prevent transmission of germs between your finger and his anus. Start slowly when you penetrate him with your finger, building up to feeling his prostate area and stimulating that. Or use an anal vibrator on him while you continue sucking, licking and kissing his penis. If he's into a little of Anal-play, he'll find your pro-job amazing!

Of course, he can return the pleasure and give her the equivalent pro-job. When he goes down to give her oral sex he can also stimulate her anus if she wants.

More sensational suggestions

MAKE YOUR MOUTH SPARKLE
Why not add a mouthful of bubbly when you suck his penis to give him an extra tingling sensation. Or get the same sensation by putting a little toothpaste, mint or Alka-Seltzer in your mouth before you suck his penis or kiss her clitoris. Your partner might love this sparkling, tingling sensation.

RUB A DUB DUB
You never know, but with this self-pleasure technique he may get incredibly aroused by your rubbing action. Many women masturbate by simply putting a cushion between their legs and rubbing through this padding with their hand. This gets them off because they have a sensitive clitoral region and don't like direct contact. You can get the same sensation by rubbing yourself silly on his thigh if he's too tired for sex.

PEARL NECKLACES AND OTHER SEXY STUFF
During Sex-play, many couples take things a step further and start to sex-periment, which is a fantastic thing to do. Men in

particular get carried away during the blow-job or a pro-job and ask if they can indulge in something like giving her a Pearl Necklace, where he pulls out of her mouth and ejaculates over her neck and décolletage. Sometimes this is accompanied by a little role play. For example she may be doing the role of sex slave and he's the master whose doing "as he pleases with her." Go on—feel free to get a little dirty with things like this.

FEMINIZING HIM

Gender-bending is more popular than you'd think between couples. Often, gender-bending goes hand-in-hand with some Bondage-play where the submissive and dominant roles get changed around a little. Once a man gets over his anxiety of being seen to be gay (many straight men have this anxiety!) he often relaxes and enjoys being feminized.

Many women get turned on by the idea of feminizing him. There's something about this unexplored territory that seems daring and exciting. A good way to get him to relax about it the first time you feminize him is to create a fantasy around it where you dominate him insisting that you get to feminize him. You can always build up gradually, beginning with putting a little of mascara or lipstick on him before you have sex. Or spoil each other with one of my suggestions in the Seduction chapter, like painting each other's toenails.

Once he's comfortable with this sort of feminizing take it a step further and ask him to slip into your silky panties. Begin by rubbing the silky fabric up and down his stomach and genitals. Take this Sex-play, as far as you like and he might just end up in your stockings, corset and miniskirt. As with any more adventurous Sex-play listen to his worries and anxieties. You must respect how far he's prepared to go.

LIPSTICK

While you've got your lipstick out for him why not ask him to trace your lovely hot pink or deep-red lipstick around your nipples. Let him swirl the creamy lipstick around them. Then he can gently massage in the color highlighting your nipples. It'll add a little color to your foreplay!

ADRENALINE BUZZ

I've always recommended doing an action sport or watching a scary film before sex since this means your body's primed with adrenalin to add to your natural-nooky buzz.

THICK-SKINNED

As I mentioned, men have sensitive skins, but on the whole they have half as many skin nerve receptors as women do. Some men complain that they just can't get aroused by touch on their skin during foreplay. One technique that works is to have raunchy sex on the carpet with him on the bottom as the rubbing of the carpet stimulates his skin. After that, his skin may feel more sensitive to touch!

GOING COMMANDO

Many couples get excited by having a private joke on the go when out. One simple suggestion that can have a sensational effect is for both of you to go commando—without pants or panties for an evening out. For example, as you both make small talk at a party no one will guess that neither of you are wearing underwear. Have a secret code that gives the sign to meet up in the bathroom for a quick and naughty grope or screw! Then innocently rejoin your friends. Or out at a restaurant, seat yourselves next to each other so you can have a little feel of the other's naked genitals. One of you may use this as a little surprise by innocently announcing over dinner (or wherever) that you don't have any on. Have fun with it!

For some other secret sex behavior why don't both of you go out with matching butt plugs for dinner with friends? Or make it even more daring and do this during a business dinner. If you find a butt plug pleasurable, as you occasionally squirm they'll never realize it's because you're feeling stimulated!

Another sneaky sex secret is for you two to go out using a remote-controlled vibrator. She has the vibrating end in her panties while he has control of the remote. She'll never know when he's going to choose to turn it on for her to get a sneaky little vibration! Just don't do it when she's carrying a tray of drinks back to the table.

THREE-WAY OR GROUP SEX

More couples seem to be indulging in three-way or group sex with one survey reporting nineteen percent of people keen to try it. Certainly it's come out of the closet and people are more willing to talk about their experiences of it. There are some definite ground rules if you're going to try it successfully. Do I have to tell you that no one should be pressured into this? I hope not!

- First off, you both have to want to try it.
- Second, you need to agree how to go about it—for example, will you check out contact magazines or go to a local swinging party?
- It's important to agree on ground rules. Some couples say, for example, that oral sex isn't allowed as they see it as such an intimate experience.
- You also need to agree on how to handle jealous feelings.
- It's important that you two have excellent communication with each other or it's easy to get into a jealousy or insecurity-type situation.
- Another issue that arises is whether you have sex with the same third party, or do you always look for new partners? Some people who indulge in three-ways or group sex like to meet up with the same set of like-minded people. Others get concerned that new relationships might be formed by this, which could

threaten the original couple's relationship. They prefer to always seek out new partners.

- You have to be prepared that if you try it and one of you doesn't like the experience, that you'll agree not to do it again so that one person isn't under any pressure.
- You should agree to "debrief" after such an experience to check how each other is feeling.
- Finally, you should set some ground rules about any additional contact with any of your new sexual partners, for example, no phone calls to them.

DOGGING

Dogging follows on from three-way and group sex. As mentioned, this is driving out to secluded locations and either watching others have sex in their cars, allowing them to watch you, or having group sex with additional partners. There are all sorts of dogging websites that will give you directions to where this activity takes place. There are some basic rules that apply to dogging, such as turning on the internal light in your car meaning you're happy for people to watch you.

FLASHLIGHT FANTASY

Moving from car lighting to flashlights, here's an idea for some childish fun. All you need is a flashlight for this one. Take the flashlight into bed with you. This allows you to get a fantasy going where one of you plays "explorer" under the sheets. Once down there under the dark covers, you turn on the flashlight and get to examine closely whatever you find. The one without the flashlight has to spread their legs letting the explorer examine you—but only if they agree to kiss and lick whatever they find.

WHOLE BODY ORGASM

According to Tantric sex practices, you can experience a powerful "whole body" orgasm together by following these tips. First off, as you approach orgasm you actively try to relax your major muscle groups. This is the complete opposite of what we usually do when we build to orgasm, which is to tense our muscles during thrusting activity. Secondly, you actively slow down and relax your breathing, which is the opposite again of what we normally do and that is to quicken our breathing as we approach orgasm. Next, you two should gaze into each other's eyes to give each other the support to keep your breathing and muscles relaxed. It can take practice but if you can reach orgasm while relaxed in these ways, it can be incredibly powerful.

PULSATING THE PC MUSCLE

Another advanced penetrative technique for added enjoyment is for you both to pulsate your now stronger PC muscles (because you've been doing your PC muscle exercises every day!) during penetration. For example, if she's on top, and you're gazing into each other's eyes, and she starts pulsating her vaginal muscles while he starts his PC muscles it's incredibly sensual.

AIRBED ANTICS

This might be best for some summer sex, unless you have a very warm bathroom. First get in a sudsy bath and have fun lathering each other up. Have an airbed blown up and ready to get on. Then you slip out of the bath to make love on it. As you're covered in shower gel or bath oil, you'll continue to slip and slide on the airbed.

YOUR SECRET SEX SIGNATURE

Everyone should have their own secret sex signature. This is something you do very well and can call your own. It can be any sex technique. For example, it may be a particular type of kissing or touching you've done and lovers have told you how fantastic it feels. And now that you've seen all these additional and more-advanced suggestions, perhaps it'll liven up your own sex signature. Maybe at this point you don't think you have a special technique all your own. But whatever you do well you can learn to perfect. Be creative with it and make it your very own sex signature.

I hope this chapter has given you loads of creative ideas. From my tips and suggestions, you should feel free to develop them and add your own twists and turns. That's what advancing your sexual knowledge and technique is all about; again it's all about keeping an open mind and open attitude.

Once you've taken your Sex-play into new territory it's easier to see how a long-term relationship can stay lively. All it needs is for you to throw in a new technique or suggestion every two, three or four weeks. One important consideration to bear in mind though is that sometimes when you push the limits a little with your lover you then need to come down gently. So don't forget that lots of kissing, cuddling and reassurance can go a long way. It will also mean that they are more willing to try new things again in the future because you've made it a complete experience. It's time to turn our attention to other things that can stimulate your sex life—lotions, potions and playthings!

TEN

Sensational Lotions, Potions and Playthings

Since there are so many things I could include in this chapter, I'm going to present them to you in a simple list form. First I'll include aphrodisiacs (the lotions and potions) and then the sex toys or playthings in a sexy review.

The list is not in any specific order and it certainly doesn't mean that something listed at the top is necessarily better than anything that comes at the end. I want you to continue revolutionizing the way you think about your sexual enjoyment in this chapter. Keep an open mind to playing around with things that you might not normally purchase. Sex toys and aphrodisiacs simply enhance your pleasure; they don't replace your partner or other things you enjoy.

Before we start though, it's time for a word of warning. Some people (both men and women) are threatened by the idea of using sex toys. Usually, with women, their fear revolves around the "unknown" if they haven't used a sex toy; or they have the misguided belief that the man has some sort of perversion if he's into using sex toys. When it comes to men, they often feel threatened that they won't "be needed" if their partner gets a lot of pleasure from a sex toy. As with introducing any new Sex-play, be aware of your partner's potential anxieties, insecurities and inhibitions. This means that you don't run back from the adult shop, dash in your front door and whoop for joy while clutching the amazing sex toy you've purchased that's going to make you feel more pleasure than anything you've ever tried! No, you wouldn't do that would you?!

Introduce the idea of buying an aphrodisiac or a sex toy in a confident and caring manner, particularly if your lover is a sex-toy virgin. Sound out your partner on their feelings, and if they're hesitant, you should have the skills by now to ask them why they're hesitant, in a way that gets honest information from them. Also a good way to get them on board for a little sex-perimentation with sex toys is to emphasize how much pleasure you want to give them with it.

If they still think you're being a little pervy, tell them they're in good company, as even the ancient Greeks used dildos made of wood and leather lubricated with olive oil. You can also throw in the fact that the ancient Chinese used dildos made of jade and other fine materials. The Indians made them with super-smooth ivory and the Edwardians experimented with weird and wonderful electric appliances. People fail to realize that sex toys have had such a long and illustrious history.

Aphrodisiacs

There's a long and rich history of aphrodisiac usage spanning centuries. The ancient Mexican Emperor, Montezuma, repeatedly used fifty cups daily of pure chocolate to fuel his exploits with his 600-strong harem. Cleopatra was reputed to drink a mixture of ground almonds, spices, honey and yogurt believed to be an energizing aphrodisiac.

A word of caution here—It's easy to get carried away, believing that an aphrodisiac will enhance sexual libido. Some aphrodisiacs have a little research supporting their energizing properties. However, others that promise an aphrodisiac affect may only have a placebo or psychological effect—that is, because you think it's going to work then it appears to work.

The following diverse selection of plants, fruit, foods and chemicals is renowned for varying degrees of aphrodisiac properties. I certainly can't guarantee they'll work for you. However, as well as some having fairly well-researched properties (for example horny goat weed), others may simply have properties that seduce you through your senses of sight, smell and taste.

If you're taking any medication, you should check with your doctor before taking an aphrodisiac preparation, many of which are available over the counter at health food shops or on the

Internet. Don't get overly excited and take too much as an overdose. Yohimbine, for example, can cause nausea and vomiting—not at all sexy. Don't get ripped off by Internet companies unless they're a company you know and trust.

Almonds—Contain properties said to revive flagging desire. Traditionally a symbol of love and fertility in Mediterranean cultures, almonds are baked into savories, sweets and desserts.

Asparagus—Greens are good for you! Asparagus is highly rich in vitamin E, which is necessary to keep your body in working order. And hand-feeding your lover an asparagus spear dripping with warm butter is a sensual experience.

Avena Sativa (green oats)—Sometimes, if mixed into preparations with other aphrodisiacs, this seems to boost their effects. Research seems to support the view that it boosts libido, particularly in people with low testosterone. Usually found in extract form, it may be added to food and drinks.

Avocado—These are loaded with essential fatty acids and anti-oxidants, which both help the production of sex hormones. Their smooth and creamy texture is very sensuous. The Aztecs called the avocado tree the "tree with testicles."

Bananas—As well as being great for your health, bananas are said to have energy-giving properties. As many people love them, they're ideal to share baked with honey, cinnamon and hot cream. Try spoon-feeding each other. For best effect, bake them in their skins as it's actually an alkaloid in their skin that has an "aphrodisiac" effect. This is released by baking.

Chocolate—Chocolate is rich in chemicals that give energy. The darker the variety, the better. It contains the chemical phenyl ethylamine, which stimulates the brain giving a euphoric effect and energy. It usually contains caffeine too, so potentially it is "energy giving" and mood enhancing. Certainly where mood is concerned, Casanova used chocolate "love tokens" to romance potential lovers—selecting shapes that gave some sort of unique message to them. Something very simple, like feeding your lover strawberries dipped in warm chocolate, can raise temperatures.

Damiana—One of the most popular aphrodisiacs and grown in hot countries, it has a botanical name that speaks of lust (Turnera diffusa aphrodisiaca). Mexican women have served hot drinks from damania before lovemaking that are said to create a mild euphoria. The presence of several alkaloids in it boosts circulation thus aiding sexual arousal. Sold in capsule form, or as a tincture to be taken a couple of hours before lovemaking commences.

Figs—Not only do they look gorgeous and sexy but they're full of vitamins. The ancient Greeks supposedly indulged in orgies once the fig harvest was complete.

Ginger, Cinnamon and Ginseng Powder—For 3,000 years, the Chinese have used ginger as a stimulant and other eastern cultures do the same with cinnamon. These can be baked into delicacies or sprinkled into dressings.

Gingko Biloba—Taken from trees found in Japan and China, this is well known to increase blood and oxygen flow. It is also said to enhance mood and have a knock-on effect to lovemaking. You can buy Sage Healthy Woman and Healthy Man capsules containing this and other stimulant herbs like ginseng.

Horny Goat Weed (Epimedium grandiflorum)—An herb that was traditionally seen as a sex remedy for men has now been marketed for women, too. Historically the use of this as a sexual enhancer dates back 2,000 years to the Chinese. The plants are pulverised and then sold in capsule form. As with any capsules bought from health food stores, you can take them as advised or mix them into cooking. You could also try the "Energy 69" drink which contains this and other energy ingredients.

Lavender Oil—Although renowned for its relaxing qualities, the scent is said to stimulate sexual interest. Put a few drops in your bath (unless pregnant in which case you should not use aromatherapy oils) or sprinkle some on your sheets and pillows. As with any essential oil, try a little to check skin sensitivity.

Maca—This plant is grown at high altitude in South America and it is believed to give energy and vitality.

Muira Puama—Found in the roots and bark of an Amazonian tree, this is particularly popular in Germany. Available in its raw form, you may prepare a brew with it and add to your favorite drink. It's also available in capsule form and may be mixed in with other aphrodisiacs. You can also get this in Phirago potency patches.

Orgasm "Creams"—There are various topical creams that you rub onto the genitalia which purport to increase sexual arousal and blood flow to the genitals. Many of them work with mild skin irritants like menthol-type products. These simply irritate the skin giving a sensation that some find pleasant and others find quite frankly irritating! Some contain L-Arginine, which is an amino acid known to increase blood flow to the genitals for about ten to thirty minutes each application. Always purchase from a reputable source and follow instructions carefully. Oh! Sensual Health Cream (available on the Internet) contains among other things green tea and L-Arginine, the former provides a tingling sensation and the latter helps with improved circulation. Then there is Zestra which is an oil packaged in sachets that's applied directly to your genitals. It contains natural oils that boost blood flow and stimulate nerves.

Oysters and Other Seafood—Oysters contain high levels of zinc, which is beneficial to health and energy levels. Researchers also found that they contain two chemicals—NMDA (N-methyl-D-aspartate) and D-aspartic acid that help release both testosterone and estrogen. But any seafood is fairly seductive simply through presentation and taste.

Padma 28—This herbal extract from Tibet has undergone clinical trials that found it was effective in improving blood flow to constricted arteries. Enhancing blood flow is important to achieving arousal.

Pollen Extract—You can purchase a food supplement, Femal, containing a pollen extract that relieves irritability and supposedly boosts libido.

Pumpkin Seeds—These are known for their beneficial effects for prostate health in men and production of testosterone in men. Packed with zinc they are now seen as beneficial for women too.

Rye—Not particularly sexy, but rich in energy-giving minerals that may help sexual performance.

Scents—Essential oils can play a part in setting the scene. Cleopatra (again!) used rose-scented carpets to seduce Mark Antony. Ancient Egyptians used many other fragrances in baths and oils including cinnamon, jasmine, patchouli, musk and frankincense. The Romans scented every part of their beds, walls and baths, while the Greeks were known to use floral and wine-scented oils on their bodies to heighten their sensuality. As long as you don't have sensitive skin, you can add a few drops of most essential oils into a bath, but take advice as many of them can make you sleepy or affect bodily/mental functions. Some are so potent they can irritate your skin if used without first being diluted in a neutral carrier oil. Alternatively you can burn candles scented with such oils.

Sesame Seeds—Thought to help tackle infertility, these are packed with vitamins and minerals that are energy-giving.

Testosterone Creams—These come in different strengths (male and female) and are rubbed in to the skin. Some people feel surprising results.

Vanilla—Has been popular in love potions for centuries. It tastes and smells delicious and sensual and is ideal in scented candles and oils. It's a fantastic flavoring for a rich dessert to savor with your lover.

Ylang-ylang—As well as its beautiful scent, it is an essential oil renowned for its euphoric and mildly relaxing qualities.

Yohimbine—Evidently better at increasing male libido, yohimbine is a commonly used aphrodisiac in Africa and the West Indies. Scientific trials on rodents and humans have shown a positive effect from this product derived from yohimbe tree bark. It boosts neurotransmitter levels and can be brewed into a tea from its natural form or taken as a tincture available from some health food stores.

A selection of other foods that might promote either increased energy, better circulation, and/or higher libido includes—swordfish, lobster, crab, salmon and other oily fish, liver, onions, garlic, wheat germ, pumpernickel, sunflower seeds, sweet potatoes, yams, squashes, turkey, mangoes, papayas, blueberries, other dark berries, wheat grass, pomegranate, kelp and other seaweed, and sushi just because it looks sexy!

☄ SENSATIONAL SEX SECRET

After indulging in some delicious aphrodisiac desserts containing chocolate, bananas and vanilla with your lover, burn off some calories with the following positions. In the Doggy position you'll burn off 180 calories. In Girls on Top you burn off 140 calories and in the Lover's Knot you'll burn 170 calories.

SO-CALLED "APHRODISIACS" TO AVOID

Unscrupulous people will play on the insecurities many of us have in order to make some quick money. Scientists have poured scorn on various animal-based aphrodisiacs. For example, in some cultures, there's a great belief that eating the penises of animals will give you their strength. However the tissue found in those parts of an animal is not unlike that in the rest of an animal. Also, please don't buy in to claims that potions based on items like rhino horn will enhance your libido. These simply aren't based on fact. Rhino horn, for example, has about as much aphrodisiac affect as chewing your own fingernails (and it doesn't do the rhino much good either!).

Spanish Fly—Made from ground-up Cantharis beetle, almost everyone has heard of this. What they don't hear is that it should be avoided, as it may be downright harmful. Rather than making you feel sexy, it actually irritates the urinary tract, giving you an "itch." Also, it can be fatal for some people eating this, so definitely don't buy into this myth.

Toys for grown-up boys and girls

There is such a variety of sex toys available that I can only begin to outline some to get you started. This is not necessarily a definitive list but it is a broad one. I'll be giving you loads of websites at the end of the book that provide a huge selection of sex toys.

I'm going to begin my list for your sex-perimentation with pleasure-giving sex toys that don't require batteries. Then we'll work our way to battery-charged ones. Here are a number of things for your pleasure:

PERSIAN LOVE BEADS

In times gone by, these were worn by women without lovers to give them pleasure. The beads come on a string that is inserted into the vagina or anally. The beads move around as the user moves giving pleasurable sensations. These sensations are not unlike self-administered foreplay. If you have a lover, you'll find the gentle teasing sensations will arouse you for sex later on.

Many women enjoy the sensation when love beads are inserted anally and their lover penetrates them vaginally. Leave one bead outside the anus—the man can then gently pull them out during her orgasm to enhance this experience. When worn anally by men they can stimulate the prostate and also be pulled out gently during orgasm. Try the new "soft" pliable beads now available for more sensitive people.

ORIENTAL LOVE BALLS OR EGGS

These come as a pair and are made for vaginal use unlike the love beads that are often four on a string. They're a little larger but essentially give the same sorts of sensations. Whichever you prefer depends on your personal preference. For some extra pleasure, allow your lover to insert them for you, as they're less fiddly than the beads. Turn it into a game where only the two of you know they're in your vagina as you go about your errands for the day.

ANAL/BUTT PLUGS

Although originally for gay pleasure, butt plugs are enjoyed by some women and straight men too. Imagine the shape of a mini-lava lamp (remember those from the '70s?) that holds itself in place in the rectum due to the slightly bulbous end. You'll need to use lots of lubrication (as with the love beads above) as the anal passage does not lubricate itself. Coming in a range of sizes, they can be worn to give sensations before sex, during foreplay and during penetration (with a woman). There's also a "threaded" one to give extra sensation.

DILDOS

Think of a non-vibrating penis shape and that's a dildo. Some people prefer these, as they can be manipulated by your hand and unlike a vibrator that sometimes spins out of control or buzzes unpredictably, they are silent. A dildo is used to stimulate the vagina or anus by being moved in and out and around in circular motions. They can be made from all sorts of materials—some now come in very life-like plastic. If you've got the money and you want to indulge yourself, they can come encrusted with semi-precious materials from uptown adult shops.

THE ACCOMMODATOR

This is a dildo with a difference, rather strange-looking but with amazing powers to please a woman. This toy is designed for a man (or woman in a lesbian relationship) to wear while giving oral sex to her. It is a dildo shape strapped to the chin that penetrates her vagina while you lick her clitoris for double pleasure.

DOUBLE-ENDED DILDOS

These can be used in lesbian love or by straight couples in two ways: either to penetrate her vagina and anus at the same time, or to penetrate two women's vaginas at the same time, or to penetrate one of her orifices and his anus at the same time. The two people playing with a double-ended dildo need to shunt their genitals up toward each other in order for penetration at the same time to be possible. One way of making this easier is to sit facing each other and move your genitals together. If the man is going to be anally penetrated, he can lie back and twist on his side. She can remain "seated" or lie back too. Once you have the double-ended dildo in, the two of you need to move gently together with a rocking motion. This way you both feel pleasure and keep the two "heads" of the dildo inside you.

THE FRENCHY SUPER COCK

A large dildo with a big knob from which you can get good stimulation. It glows in the dark and has handy testicles you can hold on to.

SATURN CRYSTAL WAND

Gorgeous to look at, with some lovely lumps and bumps for stimulation. This doesn't vibrate but it will reach your G spot and A-zone.

STRAP-ON DILDO

As mentioned in the last chapter, it's not only lesbian couples that buy strap-on dildo harnesses, as about thirty percent are bought by straight couples. Men can play out all sorts of fantasies while being penetrated by their lover. If you feel like penetrating him with a strap-on but don't want him to feel threatened, you need to bring it up tactfully. Strap-ons require practice so don't give up with your first attempt. Begin with slow and gentle thrusts. Adjust them as you go until you've got into a rhythm. Some strap-ons designed for lesbians include a dildo for the wearer. As one woman penetrates her lover, she's also penetrated. It's important for a strap-on to fit well or else you can risk losing the pleasure in the experience.

PENILE SHAFT "SLEEVES"

A fun little item that gives extra stimulation. These are highly flexible, soft "sleeves" that may be worn on the finger or the shaft of the penis for extra stimulation of the clitoris, labia and vagina. There's an assortment of styles with a variety of ridges and "knobbles" to experiment with. Using some lubricant you can then pleasure her manually. She'll love the different sensations.

The man can slide it on the base of his penis for a different sensation during penetration. She can also try using a sleeve over two of her fingers when manually stimulating him. Don't forget that men love new sensations as much as women. You can also change the sensation of any basic vibrator by slipping a "sleeve" on it.

COCK RINGS

Cock rings keep the blood that's engorged the erect penis from flowing back out. Men who've experienced cock rings say they enjoy the sensation of the building tension while one is in place. They are slipped around the base of the penis and under the testicles holding the testicles slightly away from the body. Most men report a longer-lasting erection with extra firmness. There are all sorts of rings available but I recommend using flexible cock rings rather than those made of metal as these can stretch for easier placement. Have your lover help you put it on to add to the experience.

Don't forget to lightly lubricate it and slide it on the shaft and under the scrotum. The man should do any final adjustments over the testicles, as he'll know what feels most comfortable. Couples vary in their preferences. Some enjoy the cock ring during manual Sex-play. Others like it on during intercourse, sometimes removing it before the man climaxes. It can also be put on after penetration has started as a means of adding in extra Sex-play and slowing things down. Some cock rings have various "attachments," such as clitoral or G-Spot ticklers, or mini weights to give a pulling sensation to his scrotum. Never use a cock ring for more than twenty minutes and don't worry if the penis looks darker during this period from the collected blood.

MICRO RABBIT STRETCH COCK RING

A great sex toy for couples, it's waterproof and made of stretchy silicone with a multi-speed clit-tickling rabbit.

LABIAL SPREADER

This is something deliciously different and particularly good for the woman who is a little exhibitionist or for the man who's a little voyeuristic as it opens her up. Fantastic for sensational oral sex and can be great fun for Fantasy-play. She can play the "maiden" who's being "tormented" by an evil knight. There are straps that fasten around her upper thighs and little padded "grips" that hold the outer labia open. She gets to decide how "spread" she is, by opening and closing her thighs. With her labia spread open, her sensations are increased, as is the visual stimulation he gets. There are two real benefits besides these. Her hands don't get in the way of him giving her oral pleasure, as she doesn't have to hold herself open. Also he doesn't have to use his hands to hold her open either so they are free to stimulate her in other ways.

CHASTITY BELTS

Truly a sex toy with a difference, you can get up to all sorts of fantasy games with one of these. Some of them are beautifully made chastity belts from specialist fetish shops and others come from standard adult shops.

Toys that go "vrrrrooom!"

As there are so many styles, sizes and colors of vibrators to choose from you no longer need to buy the awful lurid-orange plastic variety that dominated the sex-toy market from the '70s onwards. A lot of finesse goes into contemporary ones utilizing more natural colors as well as artistic shapes. There are also some quite elegant and even space-age looking vibrators around.

Not only can lovers have fun with vibrators but they're ideal for masturbation (even mutual masturbation!) and I strongly advise women who've had difficulty reaching orgasm to try using a vibrator. Sex therapists recommend experimenting with vibrators in a leisurely and relaxed way. This allows you to get to know your own sexual responses. You don't need my permission to try the following!

FINGER-TIP VIBRATORS

Let's start small but perfectly formed. These come in a few variations that are slipped on to his or her finger and used to vibrate around the clitoral region. But don't stop there, as they feel fabulous on the nipples, the perineum and elsewhere too!

THE ZING FINGER

Guaranteed to give you a zing when you use this finger-sized vibrator.

THE FUKUOKU FINGER MASSAGER

A great example of the above with three different sleeves for varying sensations.

THE FUKUOKU GLOVE
Slip five fun-filled vibrating fingers on to your hand!

CLITORAL TICKLERS
Sometimes attached to regular vibrators or on their own, these vibrate but also have little attachments for added pleasure. Some have little "knobbles" of feather-like ticklers for her clitoris.

G ART BULLET
This is a vibrating bullet that has a clitoris-shaped cut out. Typical of many of the bullets, it has different vibrating and pulsing options.

G-SPOT AQUA VIBE
For bath-time bliss, this G-Spot stimulator is waterproof. It's got the "come over here" crooked-finger design and with multi-speed settings you can go for a very subtle to more powerful vibrations.

BENDABLE VERTEBRAE VIBE
Its bendable quality makes for perfect G-Spot stimulation. If you can ignore the rather lurid colors, you'll have fun with it.

VIBRAEXCITER
This is a fun mobile accessory that's connected to a bullet vibrator. You can have it so that it starts vibrating when your mobile rings. Interestingly, the vibrations last as long as your phone call does. It also vibrates for twenty to thirty seconds when you receive a text.

VIBRATING ROCK CHICK

This is quite an ingenious shape that stimulates the G Spot as well as your clitoral region at the same time. The vibrations are subtle so it may not be suitable for a woman who likes a strong vibration.

THE JESSICA RABBIT OR PEARL RABBIT

Rather strange looking, but once you try it you'll probably love it. Not only does the main vibrator penetrate the vagina but the little ears of the rabbit vibrate either side of her clitoris.

MULTIPLE VIBRATORS

There are now some mind-boggling vibrators available that have anal, vaginal and clitoral stimulating "heads" all on one toy. These are said to yield a complete sensation experience, but some women may find stimulation of all three zones at once overwhelming.

THREE-WAY RABBIT

A popular version of the multiple vibrator, this tickles your clitoris and stimulates your vagina but it also stimulates your anal area. Although it looks pretty hideous, like a lot of the rabbit toys it can certainly hit the spot.

G-SPOT VIBRATORS

These have a convenient bend in them for stimulating the "front" wall of the vagina and capturing the elusive G Spot. Some are on a "wand" with a vibrator at the end while others are thicker. Many women swear by these and you can arouse him by kneeling on your hands and knees and allowing him to vibrate you from behind.

THE PROMISE VIBRATOR
This one is curved just right for G-Spot stimulation.

LIBERTE
This vibrator has wonderful sleek contours designed to hit the G Spot. Mind you, it can vibrate quite powerfully!

CLITORAL/PUBIS VIBRATORS
Slightly egg-shaped or flat, these "sit" on the pubis/clitoral region and pulsate. They feel fabulous in a teasing sort of way. She'll be ready for penetration after some time spent with this.

"BULLET" STYLE VIBRATORS
These are smaller (and travel easily!) but still feel particularly nice around the clitoral region, down the labia and perineum. They may also be used for Anal-play but mind the hygiene message!

TONGUE VIBRATORS
For fantastic oral sex sensations, these clip onto your tongue if you're giving the oral sex. Your lover then gets a fantastic vibration as well as your lovely wet mouth!

B-DOYNG

The personalized vibrator that you can get with your own filthy saying or message branded on it. Made with Vido technology, its pulses increase the tighter you hold it. For many women this is perfect as the nearer they come to orgasm the more intense the stimulation they need.

VIDO V8

A silicone toy made with Vido technology (just mentioned) it responds to you clenching. It will make your Kegel exercises go with a bang! You can charge it with your mobile-phone-style charger. It has a cylindrical carry-case that's very sleek and attractive.

PELVIC TONER

Not exactly a sex toy but definitely a must to keep your vaginal muscle in tone.

HI-TECH VIBRATORS

There are now some incredibly "life like" vibrators that feel very skin-like. Watch out for vibrators that are made from Technoskin and UR3 materials.

HARNESS-STYLE VIBRATORS (THE BUTTERFLY)

A fantastic device once experimented with and positioned how she likes it. Strapping on to the thighs, it has a central flat vibrating area that is positioned over her genitals. It can yield fabulous sensations if he concentrates on her other erogenous zones while this is vibrating.

HARNESSES FOR HIM

There are a number of vibrators that are held in place with flexible straps being slipped over his penis and testicles, which have "attachments" for vibrating against her too during penetration. Some are flexible with little loops to slip in a vibrating "bullet" for her. Others have clit-stimulators of varying designs.

BODY MASSAGERS

There are a variety of wand-type body massagers that can be used for more than just backache! Giving wide, sweeping coverage they feel fabulous across the pubic region and down the inner thighs, across the genitals and the buttocks.

GLOW IN THE DARK

For those of you with body-shy lovers, introduce them to a glow-in-the-dark vibrator that you won't lose in the sheets.

EXTRA STIMULATION

Many women claim to be brought to a pre-orgasmic state by the Slightest Touch System. By attaching electric pads to your ankles, the current sent up to the pubic nerves evidently stimulates the pelvic region. However, this is debated by doctors and may be a placebo or simply a soothing effect these women are experiencing. Another electrical stimulator in development was originally devised for pain treatment. This is now currently being looked at and who knows if it will be ready by the time *365 Erotic Secrets for Sensational Sex* is published?

LET'S GET SERIOUS

When researching a cure for back pain, one doctor found that an electrode surgically implanted into the spinal column allowed women to turn themselves on by remote control. This has been called the Orgasmatron. Obviously, this is only appropriate for women with nerve damage, for example.

♭ SENSATIONAL
SEX SECRET

Why not slip a vibrator between the two of you while you're having penetrative sex? Move it around until at least one of you is enjoying the extra stimulation.

MULTIPLE PLEASURE

Research shows that a woman is more likely to enjoy a second or multiple orgasms when she receives different stimulation than the first time around. This is another good excuse to use vibrators (as if you needed one!). Once she's had an orgasm from manual, oral or penetrative sex, you could then try using a vibrator to give her new sensations for a second orgasm. As always, please do not buy into the myth that if you don't have multiple orgasms that as a woman you're a failure. You're not! Better to have one good orgasm than many smaller ones.

ᴸ SENSATIONAL
SEX SECRET

Many men are too shy to say they'd like to feel your vibrator running up and down their perineum and anal area, so why not suggest it yourself? Or take the lead and give him good vibrations by buzzing down and around his genitals and over his perineum. If he likes anal stimulation, use a separate toy as mentioned.

Sensational common sense

Don't forget you shouldn't use a vibrator for more than twenty minutes on one area, as you can over-stimulate it.

It's terribly important to use good sex-toy hygiene. Follow the manufacturer's instructions when washing them after use. If you only have one sex toy and want to share it then wash between use or cover it with a condom during use to keep things even cleaner. As mentioned in the passage on anal sex in the last chapter, you must keep anal toys separate from vaginal toys. Ideally, keep your toys separate from your lover's toys. Why not invest in two different bags for yours and for theirs? It's also important when using lubricants to choose water-based ones that won't breakdown the surface of your plastic-based toys. Also there are hygiene considerations.

Warning! When using any vibrator for anal pleasure—even if specifically designed as an anal vibrator—ensure you don't let go of it and "lose it." Believe me, from talking to hospital doctors, I know that they can travel far into the colon and continue to vibrate, necessitating a trip to the hospital.

Sensational extras

SUSPENDED HARNESSES

There are some great ceiling-mounted harnesses to be bought if you want to spend a little extra money. These do aim for suspension with comfort: They usually have multiple adjustable straps, and the harness suspends the woman over her lover. They can either have penetrative sex or fantastic oral sex. With a touch of the hand you can turn the harness that allows the man a different access point.

It's reasonably comfortable for him and very exciting for both. It's absolutely imperative that you follow suspension instructions carefully so it doesn't get pulled out of the ceiling. Another version of this is the Thai Basket that's also suspended above a bed or floor. She sits in the basket that doesn't have any "weave" in the center of the seat. This way there's access to her vagina and anus.

PRIVATE POLE DANCING

With Pamela Anderson leading the way, many couples are erecting poles in their bed or playrooms. You can practice your pole dancing (remember the stripping instructions) and then flaunt yourself. Great for indulging in fantasies where you work in a pole-dance bar and roleplay he's a customer who can't resist you even though it's against the club rules!

HOME PRINTER

Once you've taken those hot shots of each other you may want to invest in a home photo printer.

WHIPS, CROPS, MASKS AND OTHER NAUGHTINESS

As mentioned in the last chapter, there is a huge variety of bondage and domination paraphernalia available. All you need to do is decide the sorts of things you want to use. Relevant websites will be listed at the end of the book.

This chapter should have given you an idea of the sort of things you can have fun with. I've left out sexy gear because there's such a vast array of fetish items, sexy lingerie, etc, available that it's best you check out the websites that'll be provided.

The point of all this is to delve in and out of these little ideas for toys, playthings and "potions" that can add to your lovemaking. Also, when it comes to giving little gifts and presents, you can't beat getting creative and choosing a sensual toy or an aphrodisiac for your lover. Such things help to keep things lively between you. When choosing an erotic gift always try to personalize it with your lover's interests in mind. It's time for more fun and games now.

ELEVEN

Sensational Sex Games

B y now, your mind might be filled with sensual ideas and your cupboard bursting with sex toys, so you might just want to add in a few kinky games to play. I firmly believe that people forget that sex should be fun. People get incredibly serious and concerned about it. There's nothing wrong with being frivolous, frisky, flirty and funky when it comes to the game of lust.

If you can laugh in bed, either because you've made a funny (and perhaps embarrassing!) sex noise, one of you is a little ticklish, or you've just had some fun and games, then that's a fantastic thing. What I find, though, is that it is those who are the most inhibited who would dearly love to lighten up a little when it comes to sex. They scoff at or dish scorn on the idea that you could play a sex game. If your lover's like this, ask them to indulge you. Tell them you take full responsibility if it all becomes a complete joke. Once you've taken the focus off a lover who's a little inhibited, you might find they open up and enjoy a few sexy antics.

Another way of loosening up a lover who is a little inhibited is to take sex off the agenda and instead go out and do something fun and childish. Go to your local park and swing together on the swings. Rent a favorite DVD from your childhood. Sit back and watch with a bowl of popcorn. Go to a comedy night. Anything that gets you laughing and feeling less inhibited together. Connecting in little ways like this, it will help you to let go when it comes to sex. This is part of my revolutionary approach to sexual fulfillment, where it's important you approach the whole enjoyment of your relationship rather than focusing on sex as a separate entity. Sex and relationships don't work like that. Enjoyment or lack of enjoyment in one affects the other and vice versa.

The other point I'd like to make before I outline some games for you to try is to remember never to laugh at a lover. That's a sure-fire way to make them feel they can't let go and get involved in something that seems a little edgy or different. Instead, laugh with a lover, or laugh at yourself—but never at them!

Please feel free to tailor the following games in any way you like. You can also invest in a variety of adult board games but some of them are quite pricey. Instead put your imagination to the test and enjoy the following.

Here's a selection of games to enjoy and hopefully encourage you to dream up some truly sensational Sex-play of your own.

Play those games

COME AND GET IT

To get you started in thinking about being inventive, try this simple "game." One of you waits quietly (but ready for lust) perhaps sipping a glass of wine while the other gets ready for lovemaking. The twist is that they get to choose the room and location (be it in the bath, bedroom, over the kitchen counter, on the floor, on the sofa, etc.) as well as the bits and pieces to go with some luscious lovemaking. For example, they may run a steamy bath lit by candles with a new waterproof sex toy. They then call you on your cell and tell you where to "come and get it!" This is the sort of Sex-play that you can take turns in doing the choosing. The next week (or day, or month!) the other selects the place and the bits and pieces.

I SPY

A little bit of antics to get your sex games started. Taking the traditional "I Spy," you are going to transform it into something a little saucy. One of you goes first and gives a clue that your lover has to guess. It's important to be creative. As in I Spy, you give them the first letter of a word of something you can see. For example you might say, "I spy with my little eye, something begin-ning with B." They might guess "Breasts" when actually you were thinking of "Butt." Go for it and use all the rude slang names you know for erogenous zones and the genitals. If they can't get it right, you have to guide their finger or lips to the correct area. Once there, they've got to give you a little little of foreplay!

WHAT IS IT?

This is a sensual little game that really is a sensational foreplay technique in disguise. Decide who gets to be blindfolded and lies down. The other rubs lots of lubricant all over their body, includ-ing fingers, toes, chin, tip of nose, genitals, etc. Next you touch the blindfolded partner in an erogenous zone. They have to guess what you are touching them with! Trickier than you think when you're blindfolded. A lubed-up elbow feels very much like a lubed-up palm of the hand. If they guess correctly, they are allowed to ask to be touched there for however long they want. If they're wrong, they swap places.

STRIP POKER

A classic game to build sexual tension where the loser bares all and the winner sees all. Very timely, seeing how poker is so pop-ular. You can do this with a card game of your choice, for example even strip chess, monopoly, etc., if you're not poker fans. Each time one of you loses, you have to forfeit an item of clothing. There can be no cheating and you both have to abide by the rules! Once one of you is completely naked you could carry on playing with sex toys. Each time someone loses, they have to stimulate the other with a sex toy for a few minutes.

X MARKS THE SPOT

Definitely one when you've had a drink or two and you're ready to laugh. Take two large pieces of graph paper, one for each of you. Take turns lying down and with a felt-tip pen, your lover outlines your body, then you outline theirs. Mark with an X each of your favorite erogenous zones. As with a grid, mark numbers down the side and letters across the top. Take turns calling out grid references for your erogenous zones and your partner has to stimulate that area.

TRUTH OR DARE

The perfect excuse for a little sex-perimentation. In your youth you probably played truth or dare but I hope not like this! Set the scene with some soft music, sexy lighting, and cuddle up on that sofa. On separate sheets of paper each of you write out five "dares." Fold and place in a bowl. Dares give you the opportunity to experiment, as they can be anything you want. For example, you might want to try something new like anal rimming (don't forget the dental dams or plastic wrap), or a little raunchy like having to "pee" in front of the other. It might be something like having to do a lap dance to music or letting them play "flashlight fantasy" all over your body, etc. Make the dares a mix of pleasurable or naughty. Now that you're ready, you take turns asking each other intimate questions, for example, "What's the sexiest fantasy you've ever had?" or "Where's the most unusual place you've ever had sex?" If the question makes you cringe and you don't want to answer, you have to choose a dare out of the bowl. My only word of warning is that if you decide to tell the truth about a question, make sure it's not anything that would upset your lover.

MUSICAL CARESSES

This playful activity will drive you both crazy. Toss a dice to see who gets to be in control of the music. Highest number wins the toss. Keep the CD player control at your side. When the music is playing, you can dive in for some foreplay or oral sex. But the person in control can turn-off the music at any point and you both have to stop touching each other. Tease and tempt the one who doesn't have the controls. Perhaps tell them that if they do X, Y or Z to you, you'll let the music play on and on until you're both satisfied.

MUSICAL POSITIONS

Carrying on the musical theme, this time you get in bed and are allowed to stay in one penetrative sex position for as long as the music is playing. When the music stops he has to withdraw and when it starts again you have to get into a new position. You may end up battling over who gets control of the CD player! But this is a fantastic way to force yourselves into new positions rather than staying in your favored few.

CONTROL YOURSELF!

This is a little of a challenge to holding back and controlling yourselves. Take a notepad and each of you has to write down what must be controlled when a pre-agreed code word is said. You'll take turns saying the code word. For instance, when he goes down on you he's only allowed to give you ten licks when you say the code word. Or when you say the code word during penetration, he's only allowed five thrusts and then he has to withdraw. Ultimately, the winner is the person who can best control themselves and abide by the code words. The point of this little game is to learn how to slow things down, which can be a fantastic help if one of you has the tendency to rush sex. You may also build sexual stamina.

MYSTERY SEX

We all harbor secret little things we'd like to try. Get a notepad and both of you write down three sexual things you've always wanted to try. These are folded, marked with your initials and mixed up. Having agreed in advance that you'll be open-minded about what the other has suggested, you each draw out one of the other's suggestions.

SLIPPERY TWISTER

Everyone loves the game Twister, but do this either naked or in your skimpiest and sexiest gear. Lather each other up with loads of massage oil so that you slip and slide as you play classic Twister. Or you can take turns with each having to do sexy things to each other rather then moving into another position. For example, reach out and caress an erogenous zone or plant a naughty kiss somewhere when it's your turn. Eventually you'll collapse into a heap and undoubtedly some interesting sex.

FORFEIT

You'll have to be feeling light-hearted and flirtatious to be in the mood for this little bit of fun. It is quite sexy, though, and you can plan to play it but in a spontaneous way. For example, if you're cuddled up with a glass of wine and decide to get sexy this is a good way. You take turns miming something that the other guesses. If they don't guess correctly, they have to make a forfeit—maybe strip off an item of clothing or perform a sex act. A good example is that she may appear to be miming oral sex but she's actually miming sucking his finger. So it can be a little little challenging but always fun.

PORN STAR

Using a camcorder or a cell phone, or at least a Polaroid camera, decide who is the porn director and which one of you is the porn star. Get into the action while the filming is running and then sit back and enjoy the show. For your personal security, erase any videos or destroy any photographs after your porn-star antics.

SEXY DICE

An easy little game of fun. You can buy commercial "lovers' dice" that are already labeled (instead of numbered) on each side. One dice has different erogenous zones on each side and the other has actions to be carried out on each side, such as kiss/nibble. But you can make your own and together agree a list of what the six numbers on a die represent, for example, "1" = breasts, "2" = genitals, "3" = bottom, etc. The second die again needs to be defined but this time the numbers represent an action/activity, for example, "1" = a lick, "2" = a thrust, "3" = a rub. Next you take turns throwing the two dice together. The one who throws the dice combines the erogenous zone and activity from the two dice to do for their lover, such as lick their lover's nipples.

SEXY SPELLING

I've already suggested you try playing Forfeit and this is another guessing game. When you're relaxed, maybe flirting and enjoying a little foreplay, try this. With a lovely moist tongue, write a sexy message on your lover's body. They have to guess each letter, then they string these together to form the phrase. If they guess the phrase correctly you two get to do it. So get ready for lots of licking and lapping as you spell out those letters on your lover's abdomen, thighs, buttocks, breasts—anywhere you feel like!

STRANGERS IN THE NIGHT

We already had such fun discussing fantasies and this little game is based on the fantasy I've already recommended. This takes a little thought and creativity to turn it into a game. One lover knows the plot and the other is surprised. This is the perfect sex game to play if you two are planning some quality time together. One of you—the "stranger"—selects a fantasy to be acted out. It can be anything along the lines of strangers meeting by "accident." For example, you bump into each other in a bar or office. The other follows the stranger's lead. For example, the stranger suggests you go have "al fresco" sex in the woods, or go to a restaurant and fondle each other under the table. Take turns and swap roles the next time you play this game.

SPIN THE BOTTLE

A new twist on an old game. One of you lies down and the other lubes up your abdomen. Rub lots of something slippery all over it. Your lover takes a small, empty bottle, such as a beer bottle, and spins it on your abdomen. Wherever it points to when it stops, your lover has to indulge you with lots of kissing and licking.

KNOCK, KNOCK

Have fun deciding who's going to be the mystery visitor that knocks on the door "unexpectedly." They pretend to be someone with a purpose, for example the gas man wanting to check the meter, the door-to-door sales person, or a nosy neighbor who wants to investigate a leak. You let them in and begin some outrageous flirting. The "door-to-door sales person" says they have some interesting products to show you. Or you may bend and stretch so the gas meter man gets an eyeful while you're reaching to open up the meter box. Get carried away with the double entendres, flirtatious fondling and enjoy the moment. All these behaviors set the scene for playing a role-play sex game.

BE MY SEX SLAVE

One of you has to be the sex slave. You have to compete in a sexy and fun test where the loser becomes the sex slave. For example, time which one of you can cope with an ice-cube on their private parts the longest. The one who lasts the longest is the winner. Once the slave is decided on, the master can indulge any whim (within reason of course!) for the evening.

THE SEX-SLAVE MASSAGE

If you're getting into a little Master/Mistress and Sex-slave play, this might be time to give a fabulous Sex-slave Massage. Light some candles and pamper the Master/Mistress by wrapping them in warm towels to keep them warm. Then rub some sensual oils, which you've warmed between your hands, on to their body. Start with lovely, big sensual movements. Then, with smaller and more delicate movements, work on their more sensitive erogenous zones. Sex-periment with different touches—from your fingertips to feathers, to silky sashes, to kitchen brushes, to a vibrator, and back to your hands. Utterly spoil the Master, but when you've finished with this sensational massage you become the naughty slave! Bring the Master/Mistress to the point of no return and then refuse to let them climax. This will lead to more fun and games between the naughty slave and the Master/mistress!

SURPRISE PLEASURE

I've already recommended that you should go through *365 Erotic Secrets for Sensational Sex* together and take turns choosing new techniques or positions to try. But why not blindfold yourselves and randomly flick through this guide or an adult magazine. Then whatever your finger lands on, you two will try—or as near to it as you can. This is a great way to generate some spontaneous Sex-play.

I'M DESSERT TONIGHT!

An excellent way to rejuvenate your oral sex skills is to indulge in this. On separate sheets of a notepad write out instructions covering all types of kissing, licking and sucking. For example, you write down one type of oral play on each piece of notepaper. So you might end up with six pieces: one that says "lick," one that says "suck," one that says "nibble," one that says "blow," one that says "flick," etc. Toss a coin or decide between you who's "dessert" and who's "dining out"!

Now you need to select all your favorite foods from the fridge. If you have a sweet tooth, why not indulge it with luscious things like whipped cream, caramel and chocolate sauce, and maybe some chopped nuts. Turn the kitchen table into a sex platform. Light the kitchen with candles, placing cushions and blankets on the kitchen table for comfort. You can cover them with a sheet to make cleaning up easier. Make sure your lover is comfortable lying back on the table. You dine off of them using your lips and mouth and even a spoon for extra pleasure. The feeling of your warm lips through the sauces and creams and then the cool of a steel spoon creates all sorts of wonderful sensations. Make sure your lover gets to be dessert next time you enjoy this little game.

KEEP THE SURPRISES COMING

Not so much a game, as just generally ensuring you keep the fun in your sexual relationship. You should alternate, taking turns every two weeks or so to surprise each other. The person designated to do the surprising either buys a new sex toy or arranges a hot date somewhere new and different. Try and be inventive and put some sort of price limit on the surprises. More often than not, it's the little things that don't cost much which are the best surprises.

After-play

I explained to you how important Before-play is to your relationship. The better your relationship is, the more ready you'll be for some real Sex-play. However, don't forget what I call After-play too. You've had a laugh, you've played a sex game, you're both spent and sometimes you want to deepen the moment. This is the time for a gentle touch, an affectionate hug and to whisper some loving words to each other. After-play is so important to deepening your emotional intimacy. This is the time when the bonding-hormone oxytocin is racing around your body. So use these delicious moments to enjoy the most simple and tender After-play.

I hope this selection of sexy suggestions has given you lots of ideas to continue keeping your sex life fresh. Playing sexy little games can add another dimension to your lovemaking. But you might only play a little sex-game once or twice a year. That's absolutely fine, as you should know with your revolutionary new thinking that you don't have to have sex by anyone else's rules. Set your own!

I'd like to finish by wishing you a sensational sex life! I hope *365 Erotic Secrets for Sensational Sex* has opened your mind to new ways of enjoying pleasure with your sexual partner. Try taking my Sex Quotient Quiz on the next page to find out how much you really know about you and your partner's sexual needs. Whether you're single or part of a couple, keeping an open mind to new experiences and sensations will give you pleasure and keep things fresh and ultimately fulfilling. Each one of us in a sexual relationship, no matter how long or how brief a fling it might be, deserves to be in control of our feelings and enjoyment.

Happy and sensational loving!

The SQ Quiz—
Your Sex Quotient

Take my quick quiz to work out your Sex Quotient or SQ. Your SQ will give you an idea of how well you communicate your sexual needs, listen to and understand the needs of a partner, and generally how positive or negative an attitude you have toward sex and your sexual relationship.

Read each question or statement carefully. Circle the answer "Yes" or "No" for each question or statement. If for some of them you believe you'd sometimes answer "Yes" and sometimes answer "No" then select the choice you'd select *most* of the time.

1. You <u>wouldn't</u> fake an orgasm.   Yes or No
2. You would discuss sexual issues.   Yes or No
3. You do suggest new sexual techniques.   Yes or No
4. You think a lover has faked orgasm with you.   Yes or No
5. You feel comfortable masturbating in private.   Yes or No

6. It wouldn't bother you if a lover masturbates.   Yes or No
7. If not in the mood for sex, you'd be honest
    with your lover.   Yes or No
8. You would be honest about difficult feelings
    with a lover.   Yes or No
9. You would like to be told if you're doing
    something "wrong" in bed.   Yes or No
10. You agree that people have different levels
    of sex drive.   Yes or No
11. You're open to your lover's suggestions in bed.   Yes or No
12. You accept your body, warts and all.   Yes or No
13. You're happy to share fantasies with a lover.   Yes or No
14. You're prepared to find a compromise over
    sexual differences.   Yes or No
15. You like to vary the positions you use in bed.   Yes or No
16. You try to make your lover feel good about
    themselves.   Yes or No
17. You expect to practice safer sex and would
    always suggest it.   Yes or No
18. You won't be offended if your lover said "No"
    to specific sexual requests.   Yes or No
19. Romance is important to lovemaking.   Yes or No
20. There's a place for things like "quickies" in
    a sex life.   Yes or No
21. You would be honest if experiencing
    something like premature ejaculation.   Yes or No

22. You wouldn't take it personally if your partner experienced, for example, premature ejaculation.   Yes or No

23. You would tell your partner if they were being too rough or too gentle.   Yes or No

24. Being a good lover has nothing to do with, for example, how many times you've had sex.   Yes or No

25. Sex doesn't make you feel, for example, uncomfortable, "dirty" or guilty.   Yes or No

NUMBER OF YES ANSWERS:

20–25 "Yes" answers = High SQ

You understand that sex and sexual relationships are complicated things that need openness, honesty and sensitivity to nurture and enjoy them. Look closely at the few "No" answers you have. Can you put your essentially positive attitude and sound understanding about sexual relationships to good work over these few issues? Apply any relevant suggestions from Sensational Solutions in the first chapter and from Sensational Sex Talk in Chapter 4 to these areas.

12–19 "Yes" answers = Medium SQ

You probably have a good understanding that sex and sexual relationships are complex. However, you let some inhibitions or a lack of confidence prevent you from developing a more positive attitude to them. Take each question/statement that you answered

"No" to one at a time, and think through how you can make these areas more positive. As above, use relevant advice from the passages in Sensational Solutions in Chapter 1 and Sensational Sex Talk in Chapter 4 to help you develop a higher SQ.

1–11 "Yes" answers = Low SQ

You undoubtedly have some issues with self-confidence and communication that hold you back from truly enjoying sex and sexual relationships. Don't feel overwhelmed by the number of "No" answers you selected. Instead, start building your confidence generally, so your relationships improve overall. Next, take small steps to start asking for what you'd like from your sexual partner. At the same time, let them know you'd like them to be honest with what they'd like in bed. Do this in a loving and positive way, and ask for love and reassurance from them. Agree that if you feel overwhelmed or uncomfortable with anything that you'll let them know immediately and you'll stop any sexual behavior and replace it with loving affection until you're ready to move on. Retake the SQ Quiz in three months' time.

Further Information

WEBSITES AND CONTACTS

By the time this goes to print, some of these addresses or contact numbers may be out of date. Apologies in advance for that.

A major word of warning—I can't be held responsible for credit-card fraud if, for example, you go on a website that is not secure, give your credit-card details and get ripped off. You must check if you're going to make a purchase that the site is secure at the time of use!

HELPFUL NUMBERS

National Crisis Pregnancy Helpline—800-395-4357

Planned Parenthood National Counseling Hotline—800-230-7526

Sexaholics Anonymous—866-424-8777

Couple Communication—800-328-5099

San Francisco Sex Information Line—415-989-7374

WEBSITES

Here is a tiny selection of the adult websites out there. Most of these are straightforward sites selling a range of sex toys and products. I've made a note if they're a speciality site or emphasize some other adult entertainment. (All websites are prefixed with www.)

Adameve.com

Agentprovocateur.com

Annsummers.com

Blissbox.com

Cherrybliss.com

Couplebox.com—store your private pics securely

Emotionalbliss.com

Eroticprints.org

Femmefun.com

Femininezone.com—info and advice

Fetteredpleasures.com

Glamorousamorous.com

Goodvibes.com

Hunkystrippers.com

Male101.com—about men and sex

Mencorp.com—strippers

Menforalloccasions.com—escorts

Mr-s-leather-fetters.com

Myla.com

No-angel.com

Passion8.com—erotica

sa.org—Sexaholics Anonymous

Sexchampionships.com—sex game to play online

Sexplained.com—info on STIs, etc.

Serpentstail.com—hot reading

sfsi.org—San Francisco Sex Information

Sh-womenstore.com

Skintwo.com

Thespark.com—fun site

Wickedlywildwomen.com

Willyworries.com

Other Books by Amorata Press

NAUGHTY TRICKS AND SEXY TIPS: A COUPLE'S GUIDE TO
UNINHIBITED EROTIC PLEASURE
2nd Edition, Pam Spurr, $10.00
Designed to present quick and easy advice, this book shows couples how to start improving their sex life immediately. It serves up hundreds of bite-sized tidbits that are sure to enhance and expand anyone's sexual repertoire.

THE BEST SEX YOU'LL EVER HAVE!
Richard Emerson, $13.95
Packed with a variety of new ideas to spice up lovemaking, *The Best Sex You'll Ever Have!* illustrates risque positions, fantasies, role playing, sex toys and erotic games.

THE LITTLE BIT NAUGHTY BOOK OF SEX
Dr. Jean Rogiere, $9.95
A handy pocket hardcover that is a fun, full-on guide to enjoying great sex.

THE LITTLE BIT NAUGHTY BOOK OF SEX POSITIONS
Siobhan Kelly, $9.95
Fully illustrated with 50 tastefully explicit color photos, *The Little Bit Naughty Book of Sex Positions* provides everything readers need to start using these thrilling new positions tonight.

SECRETS OF SEXUAL BODY LANGUAGE
2nd edition, Martin Lloyd-Elliott, $17.95

Shows how to take advantage of the vast world of nonverbal communication by teaching you the basic principles of sending and receiving body language.

ORGASMS: A SENSUAL GUIDE TO FEMALE ECSTASY
Nicci Talbot, $16.95

Straight-talking and informative, *Orgasms* is a girl's best friend when it comes to understanding the physical, psychological, and spiritual factors contributing to great sex and intense orgasms.

THE WILD GUIDE TO SEX AND LOVING
Siobhan Kelly, $16.95

Packed with practical, frank and sometimes downright dirty tips on how to hone your bedroom skills, this handbook tells you everything you need to know to unlock the secrets of truly tantalizing sensual play.

To order these books call 800-377-2542 or 510-601-8301, fax 510-601-8307, e-mail ulysses@ulyssespress.com, or write to Ulysses Press, P.O. Box 3440, Berkeley, CA 94703. All retail orders are shipped free of charge. California residents must include sales tax. Allow two to three weeks for delivery.

About the Author

Dr. Pam Spurr is a psychologist, award-winning radio-show host, national newspaper columnist and a sex advisor renowned for her full and frank advice. She is also the author of *Naughty Tricks & Sexy Tips*, *The Dating Survival Guide*, *The Break-up Survival Kit*, *Dreams and Sexuality: Interpreting Your Sexual Dreams* and *Understanding Your Child's Dreams*. A native Californian, Dr. Pam now lives and works in London, England, making frequent visits to the United States.